MARCO ⊕ POLO

JUL 2 1 2014

Travel with
**Insider
Tips**

AUSTRIA

Hamburg

Berlin

POLAND

Cologne   Dresden

Frankfurt

LU **GERMANY**   **CZECH REPUBLIC**

Passau   **SLOVAKIA**

Munich   Vienna

Salzburg   **HUNGARY**

LI **AUSTRIA**

CH

SLOVENIA

ITALY

www.marco-polo.com

SYMBOLS

INSIDER TIP	Insider Tip
★	Highlight
●●●●	Best of …
⊻	Scenic view
☺	Responsible travel: fair trade principles and the environment respected

PRICE CATEGORIES HOTELS

Expensive   over 140 euros

Moderate   90–140 euros

Budget   under 90 euros

The prices are for two persons in a double room per night and include breakfast

PRICE CATEGORIES RESTAURANTS

Expensive   over 20 euros

Moderate   12–20 euros

Budget   under 12 euros

The prices are for a normal main course without drinks

On the cover: Graz – historical, cultural and trendy p. 90 | Wachau – rich in history p. 71

CONTENTS

Burgenland/Vienna/L.A. → p. 64

Steiermark/Kärnten → p. 86

Trips & tours → p. 102

Road atlas → p. 130

DID YOU KNOW?

MAPS IN THE GUIDEBOOK

(132 A1) Page numbers and coordinates refer to the road atlas
(0) Site/address located off the map. Coordinates are also given for places that are not marked on the road atlas
(U A1) Coordinates refer to the street map of Vienna inside the back cover

INSIDE BACK COVER: PULL-OUT MAP →

PULL-OUT MAP

(🛏 A–B 2–3) Refers to the removable pull-out map
(🛏 a–b 2–3) Refers to the additional inset map on the pull-out map

The best
MARCO POLO
Insider Tips

Our top 15 Insider Tips

INSIDER TIP **Summer in the City**
With your feet in the sand and a drink in your hand, The Herrmann Beach Bar is the place to relax and experience the Mediterranean side of Viennese life → p. 81

INSIDER TIP **Mud-slinging**
Ultimate fun for the kids in the form of heavenly slush in the Murmliwasser near Serfaus: how about building castles and dams or doing some real mud-slinging? → p. 115

INSIDER TIP **Secret recipe**
The recipe for the scrumptious Zaunerstolle is a carefully preserved family secret in Bad Ischl: you can taste it on the Traun Esplanade – a twofold pleasure! → p. 52

INSIDER TIP **Halfway meadow**
A meadow settlement, neither high up nor deep down in the valley, is known as a *Vorsäßsiedlung* in Vorarlberg: and Schönenbach is probably one of the most beautiful of all → p. 107

INSIDER TIP **Picturesque Villgraten Valley**
The long-established Gannerhof Hotel in East Tyrol seems to have come straight out of a painting by Albin Egger-Lienz. As idyllic as it gets → p. 47

INSIDER TIP **Bargain tip**
Salzburg is an expensive spot (photo above). But you can live relatively inexpensively in the All You Need Hotel at the foot of the Kapuzinerberg → p. 59

INSIDER TIP **Up-to-date**
Hotel Daniel in Graz: a smart city hotel with urban chic at reasonable prices thanks to its 'Design & Budget' concept → p. 94

INSIDER TIP **Brilliant photo motif**
Near Kals, snap the Großglockner, Austria's highest mountain, full-frame and in all its majesty (photo below). If that's not enough, you can set off on a hike or explore an educational nature trail → p. 47

3 0053
01069
3516

BEST OF ...

GREAT PLACES FOR FREE

Discover new places and save money

FOR FREE

● *Free festival fun*

A festival pass for a one-day open-air event usually costs around 50 euros. At the end of June around 2000 artists from all spheres – rock, pop, indie, hip-hop, oldies, electro, folk music and cabaret – perform on twenty different stages three days long on the *Danube Island in Vienna*. And it doesn't cost a cent! → p. 78

● *Cardmania*

In some districts, you will be given a so-called *card* if you spend the night in one of the partner establishments. This provides discounts on many entrance fees and cable-car rides → p. 121

● *Get more out of your hike*

One often walks straight past the loveliest things without noticing them, such as a beautiful orchid or an attractive old wooden fence. That will not happen if you are accompanied by the two *Kitzbühler Wanderführer (Kitzbühel Hiking Guides)* Engelbert and Madeleine – and their tour is even free → p. 46

● *For bookworms*

Austria is a small country but it has produced many famous writers. The life and work of three of them – Robert Musil, Ingeborg Bachmann and Christine Lavant – is documented in the *Robert Musil Literature Museum* in Klagenfurt. Admission is free → p. 97

● *Swimming with a view*

Entrance to an outdoor swimming pool usually costs at least 2.50 euros. The setting in the *Strandbad Obertraun* on Lake Hallstatt, as well as directly on the Danube in the *Wachau*, is not only spectacular, it is free of charge → p. 52, 72

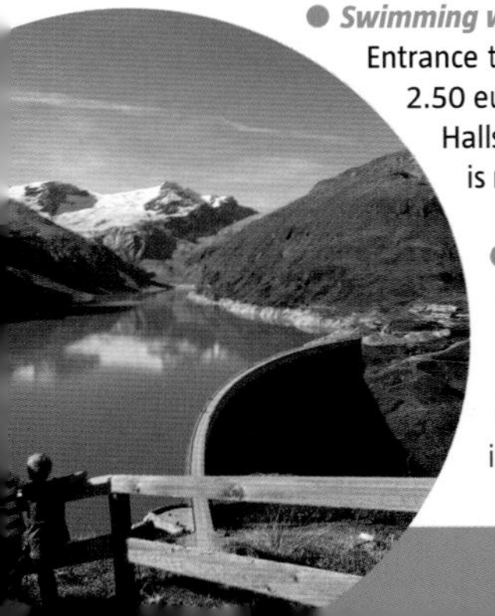

● *A miracle of technology*

A visit to the *Wasserkraftwerk Glockner-Kaprun* will not cost you anything, and you can watch how a power station works and after that learn about the most important aspects of producing electricity in the interactive exhibition (photo) → p. 62

●●●● Dots in guidebook refer to 'Best of ...' tips

● *The wine experience*

Wine growers in the east of the country have experienced a real upswing in recent years. The, model architectural setup of *Weinerlebniswelt Loisium* in Langenlois is the visual expression of this new age that has led to a marked improvement in the international reputation of Austrian wine → p. 70

● *What's that crawling or flying around here?*

In the *Alpenzoo Innsbruck*, you will see all of the animals that are native to the surrounding countryside and could be nearby — alpine ibexes, chamois, beavers, owls and some other species such as elks, wolves and bears (photo) that used to have their habitat in the Alps but have now become almost extinct → p. 37

● *Urban living room*

Austria is much more than an antiquated cliché — and you will get a feeling of the young, modern lifestyle that has now become typical of the country in the inner courtyard of the *Museumsquartier,* where not only the sofas invite you to chill out but also the frequent (free) events at which you can have fun all night long → p. 77

● *Herbed milk and alpine cheese*

There is a long tradition of cheese making in the Alps and this is especially true of the Bregenz Forest region that is famous far and wide for its tangy mountain-cheese specialities. You can buy some delicious mountain cheese in the *Käsekeller* in Lingenau, and watch the robot in charge of looking after the wheels of cheese → p. 46, 106

● *The Alps in sandals*

Normally, only mountain climbers get to see this panorama: the clear, unobstructed view of around thirty 3000-metre peaks. However, the *cable car on the Kitzsteinhorn* makes it possible for non-hikers to experience the countryside at its most spectacular → p. 62

● *Shopping for traditional clothes*

No matter whether you want the full works — a *dirndl* for the lady, *lederhosen* with a heavy jacket or traditional suit for the man — or just want to smarten up you wardrobe with some jewellery or scarves: you will be sure to find just what you are looking for in the *streets of Bad Aussee* → p. 89

BEST OF ...

● **Investigate the Big Bang**
The *Ars Electronica Center* in Linz is the place to go to find out more about the gigantic – and miniscule – secrets of the world. The fascinating interactive exhibitions are so well-organised and lucid that you might even be able to understand the research CERN is doing into the Big Bang → p. 53

● **White gold**
It would be a pity to go underground when the weather is fine but it can be fun to *visit a salt mine* in Hallstatt or Hallein when it is not quite so good → p. 52, 59

● **Underground again**
The temperature in the *largest ice cave on earth* is always only just above freezing. After your visit, it will definitely feel much warmer outside than it actually is → p. 60

● **Shelter of the glasshouse**
Relaxing in pleasantly warm water is always a great pleasure. And it feels even better if you can watch a storm raging in the mountains through the gigantic panoramic windows of the *Tauern Spa* in Kaprun → p. 62

● **Put on your wellingtons**
The other-worldly moor landscape of the *Blockheide* in *Gmünd* exudes a particularly mystical air when it is raining. This is one time when rain actually improves the atmosphere and does not make things worse → p. 85

● **Let there be light**
You will be enchanted by the light and sounds in the *14 halls of miracles* designed by the artist André Heller in Wattens. Even when the weather is miserable outside, you will experience a dazzlingly bright world in here (photo) → p. 43

RAIN

RELAX AND CHILL OUT
Take it easy and spoil yourself

● *Breakfast in the afternoon*

Sit down at a table on the terrace of one of the many restaurants at the *Naschmarkt in Vienna*, and watch all of the activity going on around you while you sip a glass of home-made peppermint tea. Make a leisurely start to your day; breakfast is served here until 4 o'clock in the afternoon → **p. 78**

● *View without stress*

Others have to sweat a lot to experience these magnificent views, but the *Großglockner observation platform* makes it possible for the less ambitious to have the glaciers at their feet without any effort (photo) → **p. 100**

● *Pamper yourself at dinner*

No matter whether you sit outside in the lovely garden or in the cosy room inside – the atmosphere in the *Weinhaus Attwenger* is always wonderfully relaxing. And the food is also excellent and not terribly expensive. An enjoyable evening is practically guaranteed → **p. 52**

● *Swim in Art Deco and Jugendstil*

If you want to spend a beautiful summer day in Baden, spread out your towel at the *Thermalstrandbad* – it offers the perfect way to sightsee and relax at the same time. Tip: the park-like section at the back of the giant area is the most peaceful area → **p. 66**

● *Successful combination*

The modern architecture of the *Hungerburgbahn* funicular railway stations in Innsbruck makes them well worth a visit. After that, you can continue your leisurely sightseeing tour by hitching a ride up to the *Nordkette* (North Chain). This allows you to admire the mountain world around Tyrol's capital city from the café-restaurant at the top without running the risk of any sore muscles → **p. 38**

● *A view from the water*

Experience the Wachau, the narrow Danube valley, from its most beautiful side: take the boat and let the vineyards and wine-growing villages drift past you → **p. 69**

CHILL OUT

INTRODUCTION

DISCOVER AUSTRIA!

Austria is a cultural treasure trove and green gem of nature rolled into one. This makes spending a holiday here so wonderful; rich cultural sites and the most enchanting countryside can be often found right next to each other – a Baroque monastery in an alpine national park, a prehistoric salt mine on the shore of an idyllic lake, a medieval castle in the middle of a dense forest. The mentality of the people living here also plays a role in making it possible to enjoy everything at leisure; the easy-going attitude of the Austrians, who do not really like to be rushed, can be very contagious.

In keeping with that, we have a valuable tip if you want to have an enjoyable stay: don't take punctuality too seriously; a quarter of an hour more or less does not make much difference to the folk in the alpine republic. It is a better idea to go with the flow and enjoy the positive aspects of this almost southern joie-de-vivre instead of being annoyed by delays. The rather fickle weather is occasionally very reminiscent of holidays in England – and the local's answer to complaints is no different. How

Photo: Pertisau on Achensee

Vienna, architecture on the Graben

could the country be so green without the rain? And, it is precisely this magnificent nature that enchants so many visitors. Austria is a small country, with an area of 32,500mi² it is only a little bigger than Scotland, but, with more than 11 million guests from abroad each year, it is number eleven in the global tourist ranking lists. However, the country with a population of around 8.4 million – about the same as London – is one of small structures. With the exception of Vienna (1.7 million), only Graz, Linz, Salzburg and Innsbruck have more than 100,000 inhabitants – around 35% of all Austrians live in one of these cities. The remainder are villages, market towns and small cities in the classical sense.

Austria has nine provinces including the federal capital Vienna and Austrians tend to have a certain amount of local patriotism. The self-image of the Tyroleans is particularly well-developed and goes so far that there is even a saying 'bisch a Tiroler,

976
The first documented mention of Austria as Ostarrichi

1282
Rudolf von Habsburg founds the 600-year reign of the Habsburg dynasty

1529 and 1683
Vienna is besieged, but not conquered, by the Ottoman forces

1740
Maria Theresia ascends the throne

1780
After Maria Theresia's death, Josef II assumes power of the Habsburg lands

1848
Franz Joseph I ascends the throne at eighteen

bisch a Mensch' (If you're Tyrolean, you're human). The view in Vorarlberg on the other side of the Arlberg, which creates a divide in the German-speaking area, is more focused towards the west. That comes as no surprise: the only other place where the dialect spoken here is understood is Switzerland! In a referendum held in 1919, an overwhelming majority of the Vorarlbergers even voted to join the confederation, but that never happened. On the other hand, things were different in the Pannonian cultural area when Burgenland decided to remain part of Austria instead of Hungary in 1921. These two smallest federal provinces are geographically worlds apart, even though they are only separated by 800km (497mi).

The people who live in Carinthia, the southernmost province, are absolutely convinced that it sunnier and more fun to live here than in the rest of Austria – something that certain populist Carinthian politicians regard with apprehension. Salzburg on the other hand has a strong clerical tradition as a result of having lived under the rule of regents who combined ecclesiastical and worldly power in one person for many centuries (until 1803). The inhabitants of the city of Salzburg are absolutely convinced that nothing in Austria can compare with the sophisticated lifestyle of their home town.

> **Salzburg lifestyle with a clerical tradition**

Of course, that leaves the Viennese utterly cold. They consider any place outside their city limits provincial; if a person from the country comes to the metropolis and his

years of age and reigns until 1916

1867
As a result of unrest, the double Austro-Hungarian monarch is proclaimed

1914
The assassination of the successor to the throne Franz Ferdinand sparks the First World War

1918/19
Proclamation of the First Republic

1938
Austria occupied by German troops

1945
The country is divided into four zones after the Second World War

dialect gives him away, he is immediately treated as a *gscherter* (dolt, boor). On the other hand, drivers with Viennese number plates have to be sure not to make any mistakes, such as driving agressively or calling too loud for the waiter, in the countryside: they will soon be dubbed '*großkopferter Weana*' (arrogant Viennese). However, this is rarely taken very seriously and, as a rule, the Austrians get on very well with one another.

> **No other country in the world profits as much from its guests as Austria**

And, they are just as friendly to tourists as they are to their countrymen; tourism generates around 5% of the gross domestic product. Per capita, no other country on earth lives better from its guests. It is not only in this area that Austria is stronger however. It is also a world leader in quantum computer research and the development of new energy technologies. Overall, the small country stands on a very sturdy economic footing and is always among the top ten in the EU.

Although EU scepticism is on the increase, the country has benefitted greatly from its membership in the Union (since 1995) and the subsequent eastward expansion. On the one hand, Austria – and, in this case, the eastern section of the country with Vienna in particular – has moved away from being on the outskirts and towards the centre of Europe. Vienna is now a hub for the new markets in Central and Eastern Europe including Russia and the former CIS and, as a result, is once again developing into a world metropolis. On the other hand, what were once less-developed regions, mostly bordering on the former Iron Curtain, have received significant subsidies that have led to some impressive results. These include the Güssing region in the south of the Burgenland that is now energy self-sufficient and the revitalisation of the moor spas in the northern section of Upper Austria. There is much more waiting to be discovered in Austria than its spectacular alpine landscapes.

Happily, the infrastructure has improved greatly in recent years – much to the joy of the guests who get exactly what they are looking for at reasonable prices: all-inclusive luxury or weeks spent in rustic huts, après-ski parties or solitary mountain tours. That has led to a few drawbacks: there is mass tourism in some places, especially in the west

1955 Austria once again becomes a sovereign state

1979 Vienna becomes the third UNO city after New York and Geneva

1989 The Iron Curtain on the border between Austria and Hungary is torn down

1995 Austria become a full member of the EU

2009 Linz is European Capital of Culture

2013 Alpine Ski World Championship in Schladming

The annual pilgrimage in the Lesach Valley in Carinthia makes its way to the Maria Luggau Basilica

of the country where tourism has traditionally played a strong role in the economy. The large number of visitors is also a burden on the ecology of the alpine region and that is why those responsible are doing as much as they can to protect the environment; of course, the conservationists think that this is never enough. But, the small country can be proud of its six internationally recognised national parks and biosphere reserves, as well as the numerous regional nature reserves and local conservation areas.

Often, the first image one has of Austria is of its mountain peaks. But, there are magnificent areas far away from the Alps. For example, the Pannonian vastness around Lake Neusiedl, the forests in the Waldviertel that remind one of Scandinavia, or the wildly romantic Danube gorge that is the Wachau, not to forget Vienna, the cultural metropolis. But of course, the mountains are the icing on the cake. There are plenty of offers available to help nervous lowlanders learn to love the

Austria does not automatically mean alpine

mountains, just as there are to satisfy the millions of enthusiastic hikers, mountain climbers, winter-sport fans and extreme alpinists. Austria easily compensates for its lack of seaside beaches with the magnificent lake landscapes in the Salzkammergut and Carinthia. The healing qualities of water also play an important role in the area along the thermal line in the far east of the country. In addition to the mountains and lakes and thousands of areas of natural beauty, culture is another of Austria's main tourist attractions. You are spoilt for choice in Austria: those who want to, can go to a first-class exhibition in an ultramodern palace of culture in the morning, work up a sweat on a mountain bike in the afternoon and then sip a cocktail in the cool shade of medieval walls in the evening.

WHAT'S HOT

1 On a tricycle

Twin Racers Mountain bikes have got some serious competition. For some years now, three-wheelers – so-called twin racers or mountain carts – have been seen racing along alpine paths. Their tyres are suitable for off-road riding and they have low seats making them safer than normal bicycles. You can hire the bikes at the *Kala Alm (Schneeberg 50a, Thiersee)* and from *Highend Rent (valley station, Marienbergbahn, Marienbergweg 9, Biberwier, photo)*.

Inland beach

2

Beach Bar Austria does not have a sea but that does not mean that you will have to do without beach bars. The music played by the DJs and the drinks served at *Jilly Beach (Hauptstr. 160, Pörtschach)* will make you think it is really summer. It also feels like the ocean is not far away in big city: the *Vienna City Beach Club (bank of the Danube between the Prater and Reichs Bridges, Vienna)* and *Powers (Rossaugasse 11, Innsbruck)* make this possible. And, the guests at the *Beachbar Bregenz (Seepromenade 2, photo)* almost believe they are at the seaside.

Lift up your eyes!

3

Vista Nature lovers may not like them but holidaymakers enjoy being able to see over wide expanses of countryside from observation platforms such as the *Dachstein Skywalk (www.schladming dachstein.at, photo)* on the Hungerkogel. It is a fact that an increasing number of platforms are being erected on Alpine peaks to make it possible for more people to get a clear view of nature's beauty and hopefully arouse more interest in the environment. There is plenty to see from the *Top of Tyrol* platform at an altitude of 3210m (10,532ft) on the ridge of the Großer Isidor and the glazed *Top Mountain Star* panorama bar *(www.tophochgurgl.com)* in Hochgurgl.

Fancy dress

Fashion Ever since an increasing number of young women started wearing their national costume as a matter of course, designers have been researching the possibilities of the style. Lena Hoschek was a pioneer in the field of those designers who are now creating modern, very appealing new versions of the *dirndl*. The mini-*dirndls* from *Ploom (Ursulinenplatz 5, Salzburg, www.ploom.at, photo)* are just as tantalizing and a little less expensive. Off-the-shoulder dresses and unusual materials such as silk brocade give the traditional garb a modern touch. Gabriela Urabl's creations are sometimes rather punk and sometimes quite cute. If you have your heart set on a *dirndl* with wild-animal patterns or gaudy colours, you will find what you want at *Dirndlherz (Lerchenfelder Straße 55, Vienna)*. Another hot tip is Susanne Bisovsky's Trachtenpunkt *(at Sisi, Vienna, Annagasse 11)*.

4

Black pudding is back

5

Culinary The country's top chefs have rediscovered the black pudding – in German 'Blutwurst' but known as 'Blunzen' in Vienna. One of them is Andreas Döllerer who conjures up culinary masterpieces made with Gravenstein apples, langoustines and black sausage in his toque- and star-winning *Döllerer's Restaurant (Am Marktplatz 56, Golling, photo)*. If you want to learn how to decorate your black pudding with potato straw at home, you can book a cookery course in alpine cuisine given by the chef himself. *Hotel Schloss Weikersdorf (Schlossgasse 9–11, Baden)* serves black-pudding parfait with horseradish foam and one of the specialities of the Viennese *Restaurant Vincent (Große Pfarrgasse 7)* is black pudding with goose liver and vinegar pears.

IN A NUTSHELL

ADRENALIN

The steeper, the better: climbing tours demanding the highest proficiency, downhill mountain bike races with 80% inclines, free-fall on your board ... The mountains tempt you to test your limits. This is a challenge those living in the Alps – men and women alike – readily take on. People who can ski before they learn how to walk properly, who clamber up the mountains before they have even heard of vertigo, have a head start on city dwellers. Those who learn how to get around in the mountains while they are children will still be able to lead the way when they are over 70. In Austria, there is a large community of extremely sporty people out and about: thousands of miles of mountain bike trails, climbing routes and *via ferratas*, rafting and canyoning trips, kayak schools, paragliding starting points and parachuting events ... The most ambitious sportspeople get together to measure their strength in their discipline in special contests that an ordinary person would consider absolutely insane. These include the *Mountainbike Trophy* in the Salzkammergut (200km/ 124mi) over narrow, slippery, stony, steep forest trails), the *Carinthian Ironman* (3.8km/2.4mi swimming and 180km/ 112mi cycling followed by a marathon race) and the *Freeride World Tour* (free-riding

Everyday life in Austria: extreme sports in summer as well as in winter, appealing, well-cultivated clichés and strong traditions

on the precipitous north slope of the Wildseeloder in Fieberbrunn/Tyrol).
Being fearless is a good way to become the nation's hero; the entire country yearns for the success of its aces in the major skiing world cup races. No football match arouses anywhere near as much interest as the *Ski Race Weekend in Kitzbühel* or the *Night Slalom in Schladming*. The ski-jumpers draw almost as many viewers to the television screens when they take part in the *Four Ski Jump Tournament* at the turn of the year, and it takes on the character of an international competition.

ALPINE HABITAT

The Alps, a mighty drinking-water reservoir and the home of around 5000 plant and 30,000 animal species, are surrounded by rich, densely populated conurbations with leisure-crazy inhabitants. Along with the Caribbean and Mediterranean, the Alps are one of the most important regions of global tourism. At times, there is almost as much activity on the Großglockner as on the Costa Brava; on fine days, a never-ending single file of alpinists make their way up the slopes. The permanently growing number of guest beds, access roads, mountain entertainment and climbing aids are placing an increasing strain on the Alps that are already the world's most extensively developed mountain region. The ski lifts and cable cars in Austria are capable of whisking more than 2.7 million people up the mountains every year; there are around 7000km (4350mi) of prepared ski slopes and hikers have more than 200,000km (125,000mi) of forest trails at their disposal.

This aggressive development cuts through and decimates valuable habitats in what is already an extreme climatic zone so that many organisms have to struggle for their existence. The problem is made more acute by the effects of the global climatic change that are particularly noticeable on the receding glaciers.

But tourism is not only to blame for the ecological problems, it is also one of the main hopes for the preservation of the Alps. Without tourism, the lack of any perspectives would lead to many local people leaving their home regions. There is usually a long drawn-out struggle between local environment action groups and economic interests that eventually leads to projects being realised to develop the environment carefully and sustainably. The natural environment is also strictly protected in Austria's six national parks. The Hohe Tauern National Park, which includes the highest peaks in the border region between Salzburg, Carinthia and Tyrol, is by far the largest.

H EURIGER

Wherever wine is grown there is also the institution of wine taverns known as the *Heuriger* or, in some regions, *Buschenschank*. These simple establishments serve their own wine and offer small, cold snacks. A classical *heuriger* is not open all year round but only during certain periods – sometimes for one or two weeks at a time; at others, just for a few days; the wine-growing regions publish calendars with full details of the participating winegrowers. If a *heuriger* is open, the owner hangs a bunch of fir twigs over the door. This traditional establishment has since developed into the so-called heuriger-restaurant with a special licence allowing it to serve wine from other growers and provide full meals. This kind of tavern also exists in those regions where cider is grown; only there, the beverage is made with apples and pears instead of grapes.

K AFFEEHAUS

Forget what you learned in German at school. In Austria, the second syllable of *Kaffee* is stressed. If you can remember this, you will find that the *Ober*, as waiters in coffee houses are called, might even take a liking to you. And, if you also know how to order – *kleiner* or *grosser Brauner* or a *Melange* – he will be absolutely delighted. A *Melange* is a double espresso with milk foam similar to a cappuccino; a *kleiner* or *grosser Brauner* a small or large espresso with a little milk (served in a tiny pot in better houses). A glass of water should always accompany your coffee. In addition to a small selection of cakes and snacks, most coffee houses also serve classical Viennese dishes at lunchtime; some of the more sophisticated establishments have a full menu all day long.

The days of the coffee-house men of letters are long gone but many writers are

The monastery in Melk is one of the country's most important abbeys

still enthusiastic coffee-house habitués. Robert Menasse, who is well known for his essays, likes to spend his time in the *Café Sperl* in Vienna and the grande dame of Austrian literature Friederike Mayröcker can frequently be found in the *Tirolerhof*. People do their work in the coffee house; business meetings are held there, contracts finalized and politics made. Sometimes, the *Landtmann* next to the Burgtheater seems to be a branch office of parliament a few hundred metres away. Other typical coffee houses are the *Central, Bräunerhof, Prückel* and *Sperl* (Vienna), *Traxlmayer* (Linz), *Bazar* and *Tomaselli* (Salzburg), and *Central* (Innsbruck). There is a wide selection of newspapers and WiFi has now become a standard service.

LANGUAGE

It has been said that Germans and Austrians are separated by the common language. Scholars of German language and literature know that 2–4% of the German vocabulary is more or less typically Austrian.

That is not very dramatic in the written language but can cause confusion in colloquial speech. For example, when a German *ausrastet* he loses his temper while in Austrian German it means takes a break, takes a rest. If he tells a little story – a *Gschichtl* – it's a lie; if he's *marod*, he does not feel well. An Austrian who is *stier* is broke; if he *stierlt*, he is poking around in somebody else's affairs. Even if you think your German is not too bad, you may find understanding the menu quite tricky; at school, you learned that minced meat in German is *Hackfleisch*, in Austria it's called *Faschiertes*; you were also taught that pancakes are *Eierkuchen*, in Austria, they are called *Palatschinken*. However there are also many regional differences: the Viennese say 'Viertel Eins' or quarter to one when they mean 12.15 but in Linz it's *Viertel über Zwölf*, quarter *over* twelve. There is another linguistic peculiarity in addition to all the fine differences; while the largest section of Austria is part of the Bavarian-speaking area, people in Vorarlberg speak Alemannic.

It is usually possible to tell where somebody comes from by his dialect.

MODERN ARCHITECTURE

In the 1960s, a group of young architects with a desire to experiment came together at Austrian universities and developed new forms and concepts in opposition to standard post-war building styles. Wolf D. Prix, Helmut Swiczinsky and Michael Holzer from the Coop Himmelb(l)au collective (1968), Hans Hollein, one of the post-modern pioneers, and Günther Domenig from what has since become famous as the 'Graz School', have also been successful internationally. The same applies to Friedensreich Hundertwasser; the man who later made a lot of enemies with his 'kitschy commercialism' was also a product of the Viennese scene. Avant-garde buildings such as Domenig's stone house on Attersee and Hans Hollein's Haas House in Vienna were built, but it was not until the 1990s that, all of a sudden, contemporary architecture could be seen everywhere and met with a positive public reception. This triggered a real boom that has continued until the present day and also provides a stage on which international star architects such as Zaha Hadid and Vito Accconti can perform. Cities and provinces opened fascinating cultural complexes, Vienna's skyline took on a futuristic appearance and even private builders have decided that they like the clear forms of the post-modern style. Vorarlberg plays an outstanding role in the area of modern architecture; very early on, the province in Austria's far west started concentrating on sustainable building and experimenting with innovative ground plans and materials. Nowhere else in the country is there such a dense concentration of exciting architecture and clever ecological design.

MONASTERIES

The prominent role played by Catholicism, which was defended by the imperial dynasty, led to most of the monasteries having a great deal of power and influence – especially in rural areas. They were centres of culture and education, as well as of agriculture and wine-growing, and have maintained this position to the present day. In spite of economic crises and the Josephinist reforms that led to the closure of many monasteries at the end of the 18th century, most have managed to survive and still exist today. This is, to a large degree, thanks to their immense cultural treasures. The Benedictine monastery St Paul in the Lavant Valley not only has a painting gallery that would make many museums envious but also a priceless collection of original documents and legal texts. The collections of art and curiosities in other monasteries such as Melk, Klosterneuburg, Heiligenkreuz, Göttweig, Zwettl, St Florian, Kremsmünster and Stams in Tyrol are just as precious. Many of the monasteries have opened their doors to those seeking rest and relaxation. The

One of the first avant-garde buildings in Vienna: the Haas House on Stephansplatz

offers range from overnight stays to working in the monastery's various enterprises. *(www.kloesterreich.at).*

RENEWABLE ENERGY

Although more than 70% of Austria's energy needs is still supplied by fossil sources, 26% is already provided using renewable sources – considerably more than the 20% targeted by the EU for 2020. On the one hand, this is the result of the country's long tradition of water power and on the other it is due to the massive subsidies that have been paid for private initiatives such as solar cells and small wind-power plants. In addition, various regions are making considerable investments in new technologies; Güssing in the Burgenland is a model district that is now energy self-sufficient and cooperates with universities on in-depth research projects. The focus is on the plentiful supply of biomass, such as trees, waste timber, green waste and straw. The Austrians have the ambitious goal of being able to cover 34% of their energy needs sustainably by the year 2020.

TRADITIONAL CUSTOMS

National costume is often a first choice for festive occasions; even for young people. Going to church on Sundays is becoming less of a reason to put on the *lederhosen* or *dirndl*, but many still do so for weddings and other solemn events. Traditions are maintained in everyday life but this is not so obvious to visitors: many Austrian are members of rifle, music and crossbow associations, form small choirs around Christmastime or see that the art of embroidering golden bonnets does not die out. Guests can get an idea of the wealth of customs in the Alps during public festivities – even though a little not-quite-genuine folklore does play a role in some of the really large events. A good way to really get to know the locals is at one of the countless fire-brigade, winegrower or church festivals that are so popular in country areas from spring to autumn. They can be a bit boisterous – but that is what grassroots, living folk culture is all about! It is only in Vienna and its surroundings that this rural way of life is no longer present in the everyday environment.

FOOD & DRINK

There is hardly anything Austrians appreciate more than a good meal. And there is nothing they find worse than a bad one. Traditionally, food was expected to taste like grandma had cooked it herself, but in recent years, Mediterranean and Asian influence have made dishes more varied and lighter.

Austrian cuisine deserves its international fame even though, strictly speaking, it does not really exist. Most of the time, people talking about Austrian cuisine are actually talking about Viennese cooking – which is very different to the regional, rural cooking found in the rest of the country. It is the cuisine of the long-gone Habsburg monarchy infused with many influences from the east and south of Europe that were subsequently perfected in the capital and residence city of the Empire to become an imperial style of cooking. It is a culinary patchwork of dishes that were cooked in all areas of the monarchy. Anything that was good found its way to Vienna and, if it was even better, stayed there. Goulash came from Hungary, many of the desserts from Bohemia and the *Wiener Schnitzel* has its origins in Milan. Meat dominates Viennese menus; sometimes prepared with great refinement and sometimes hefty. However, vegetarians will not have to starve; there are

Photo: Café Central, Vienna

Varied, hearty, delicious: for centuries, Austrians have been inspired by dishes from foreign shores

many sweet alternatives to meat on the dessert menu. These *Mehlspeisen* include all of the sweet goodies that are served at the end of a meal but are often substantial enough to be eaten as a main course: *Schmarren* (scrambled pancakes), strudel, *Obstknödel* (fruit dumplings), *Schmalz-gebäck* (deep-fried pastries), *Dalken and Buchteln* (yeast dough with a jam or poppy seed filling), and *Palatschinken*

(pancakes) are just some of the classics and many of them quite clearly have their roots in Bohemia. The strict fasting rules of the Catholic church led to these meat-less dishes also being served in the high-est circles; even crowned heads had to obey and there are reports that Emperor Franz Joseph I enjoyed them. Many re-gional specialities, most of them of rural origin, can be found on the menus in the

LOCAL SPECIALITIES

▶ **Backhendl** – crispy, breaded, tender deep-fried chicken, frequently served with Vogerlsalat (lamb's lettuce)

▶ **Blunzenradl** – fried black pudding with sauerkraut

▶ **Kaiserschmarrn** – pancake batter made with eggs, flour, milk and raisins; even better when it is served with stewed plums

▶ **Käsknöpfle** – spaetzle with tangy grated cheese

▶ **Klachelsuppe** – split pig trotters (Klachel) cooked in herb broth until they are tender

▶ **Linzer Torte** – dough made of butter, sugar, eggs, flour, hazelnuts and bread-crumbs, covered with thick layer of red-currant jam

▶ **Marillenknödel** – apricot dumplings made with curd-cheese or potato dough, sprinkled with sugar and bread-crumbs (photo left)

▶ **Palatschinken** – thin pancakes filled with jam, chocolate or curd cheese

▶ **Salzburger Nockerl** – a mixture of stiffly beaten egg white, icing sugar, egg yolks, a little bit of flour and grated lemon peel that is then baked (photo right)

▶ **Schlutzkrapfen** – Tyrolean-style ravioli with mountain cheese and served with sieved potatoes

▶ **Tafelspitz** – boiled beef, with vegetables, shredded fried potatoes and horseradish-cream

▶ **Topfenstrudel** – strudel filled with farmer's cheese; served with a milk-and-egg or vanilla sauce in some regions

▶ **Wiener Schnitzel** – veal, coated with flour, egg and breadcrumbs and then fried

provinces alongside classical Viennese dishes. The Vorarlbergers love their *Käs-knöpfle* (cheese dumplings), the Salz-burgers *Kasnocken* (cheese gnocchi), the Carinthians *Kasnudeln* (cheese ravioli) and the Upper Austrians adore dumplings in all forms. Here, one also notices that most of these dishes do without meat – traditionally, only Sunday was roast meat day. In addition, it is still common to pre-serve meat by pickling or smoking it – and bacon continues to play a big role in cook-ing today.

Austrian cooking is characterised by skilful preparation and hearty portions, and in-creasing attention is being paid to using the best products when preparing tradi-tional recipes or their more modern interpretation. The keywords are regional, seasonal and organic. 😊 Austria's structure has made it a European trailblazer in the field of organic agriculture. This is especially true of the province of Salzburg where half of the total farmland is cultivated organically. Guests become aware of that when they taste the unexpectedly high quality of the food they are served. Higher-class restaurants in particular are increasingly stressing the fact that they use organic produce – which naturally means regional and seasonal. In an effort to counter the hegemony of global, industrialised agriculture, the mountainous areas of Austria have established *Genussregionen* (culinary or delicatessen regions) that focus on products that have been grown locally. The apricots from the Wachau, asparagus from the Marchfeld, Pannonian Mangaliza pigs from the South Burgenland and the free-range geese from the meadows of the Mühlviertel are some of the most prominent representatives of this movement. If you happen to be in one of these regions at harvest time, you will be able to enjoy a great variety of local specialities in many inns and restaurants *(www.genuss-region.at)*.

The various naturally cloudy fruit juices and ciders, as well as fresh spring water, are often pleasant alternatives to over-sugary soft drinks. But, no meal would be complete without the appropriate wine to accompany it. Significant quantities of wine are produced in Lower Austria and the Burgenland, as well as in Styria and even in Vienna. The main Austrian varieties are the crisp, peppery, light Grüne Veltliner (which is actually white) and the rather substantial, dark violet Zweigelt. The particular vineyard is just as important for the vintner as the variety he has chosen to cultivate – modern winegrowers are proud that their wine displays the distinctive flavour of the earth it grew in.

Although Austria is regarded as a country of wine connoisseurs, three times as much beer is consumed there. The province of Salzburg has a long beer-brewing tradition, which has its origins in the province's monasteries, as do Tyrol and Vorarlberg. (Apple) cider is especially popular in Upper Austria and parts of Carinthia while pear cider has enjoyed an unexpected renaissance in the Mostviertel of Lower Austria in recent years.

Wherever wine is grown and cider pressed, *schnapps* is never far away. The distilleries that are scattered throughout the country produce high-proof spirits from pears, apricots, grape marc and even rowanberry (the fruit of the mountain ash) that will really fire your soul – a glass of good *schnapps* is said to help the digestion and make your view of the world clearer.

Hospitality: restaurant in Styria

SHOPPING

If you want to be sure that you don't end up with a souvenir from China, you should choose items made by hand; and, there is a wide selection of them in Austria. Cosmopolitan-style shopping is only available in Vienna. Here, the main shopping areas are in the expensive, golden horseshoe around the Graben and Kohlmarkt in the *1. Bezirk* (first district) and the more affordable Mariahilferstrasse, Europe's longest shopping street, in the sixth and seventh, where international (fashion) chains vie with old-established shops for the buyers' attention.

ANTIQUES & BRIC-A-BRAC

If you are looking for antiques or second-hand goods, you will be most successful in the Viennese districts inside the *Gürtel* and in Salzburg where a major antique fair is held every year at the same time as the Easter Festival. You will have a lot of fun rummaging through the goods at the flea market on the Naschmarkt in Vienna on Saturday and at a similar event held on the Esplanade in Bad Ischl on the first Saturday of the month.

CERAMICS & PORCELAIN

Ceramic ware with colourful stripes or dots: Gmundner Keramik is synonymous for everyday culture in the Alps. In addition to the complete range of products, the shop at the ceramics factory also sells new articles with tiny flaws at reduced prices. Pottery, too, and the Viennese Augarten Manufaktur, located in the former Augarten summer residence, is world famous for its superior-quality china.

CULINARY DELIGHTS

☺ Fresh farm produce – eggs, bacon, sausages, pumpkin-seed oil, raspberry vinegar, blackthorn brandy, apricots, poppy seed, pear cider and many other local delicacies – are sold directly on the farm, at local farmers' markets (usually on Friday or Saturday) and in smart country shops. *Mozartkugel* (sweet with pistachio, marzipan and nougat centre coated in chocolate) and *Mannerschnitten* (hazelnut wafers) make fine inexpensive chocolaty souvenirs for those at home. Apart from these illustrious names, the delicious

Something for everybody: sweet souvenirs, trendy traditional costumes and an enormous selection of ceramics and glass

creations of the pastry shops, chocolate makers, and confectioners can be found all over Austria.

GLASS & WOOD

Any well-stocked souvenir shop will have an outstanding selection of high-quality glassware but there are several good reasons for visiting a factory where these articles are produced: on the one hand, the products are usually less expensive and, on the other, you will almost always be able to see what goes on behind the scenes in firms such as B. Swarovski in Wattens, Riedl Glas in Kufstein and Stolzle-Oberglas in Voitsberg. Tyrol is not only a stronghold of glassblowing but also of wood carving where everyday objects are turned into works of art and nativity figures are carved with loving care. The INSIDER TIP 1. Tiroler Holzmuseum (First Tyrolean Wood Muse-

um) in Wildschönau has a wide assortment in its shop (www.holzmuseum.com). Further details on arts and crafts culture in Austria at: www.meisterstrasse.eu

TRADITIONAL DRESS

The *Heimatwerke* in the province capitals and specialist shops such as Lanz in Salzburg and Gexi Tostmann in Seewalchen are fine addresses. Alternatively, you can give your wardrobe an Alpine touch with a few carefully selected pieces: Steiner, the goldsmith in Bad Aussee, makes traditional-style jewellery; Sepp Wach, who prints magnificent silk scarves by hand, is at home in the same city. And, if you visit Loden Steiner in Mandling near Schladming, you will not only be able to see how the fabric is produced, you can also stock up on wonderfully warm clothes for winter (www.wollwelt.at).

THE PERFECT ROUTE

MAJESTIC MOUNTAINS

Leave Salzburg behind you for the time being and head straight to the mountains. In ❶ *Werfen* → p. 59, you will be able to marvel at the largest ice cave on earth as well as the majestic fortress with its bird-of-prey show before taking a break in ❷ *Zell am See* → p. 60. Here you can choose between lacing up your hiking boots and making yourself comfortable at the lakeside beach. Feel the fine mist on your skin at the Krimml Waterfalls and get close to Austria's highest peaks, without any effort, when you visit the Gipfelwelt 3000. Your route then takes you over the ❸ *Großglockner-Hochalpenstraße* → p. 100 to Carinthia.

SUNNY SOUTH

The ❹ *Millstätter See* → p. 100 is just one of the many Carinthian lakes where you will feel like you are really on holiday for a few hours in a fairy-tale natural setting. The gentle curves of the Nock Mountains invite visitors to take long hikes and cycle tours that end with a refreshing dip in a beautiful lake. After you have relaxed in this way, you leave the mountains behind you and head to the southern section of Styria by way of ❺ *Klagenfurt* → p. 96. You drive leisurely along the ❻ *South Styrian Wine Road* → p. 96, where you can taste the first-rate vintages in the taverns along the way and stock up on wine directly from the growers. The next destination is ❼ *Graz* → p. 90, the capital of Styria, where the pace of life has remained pleasantly relaxed. Visitors who take enough time to explore the city will discover idyllic inner courtyards where the Grazers meet for a glass or two of prosecco and to enjoy all of the good things the farmers' market has to offer.

VASTNESS AND THE METROPOLIS

A lengthy drive through the spa district leads over Oberpullendorf and ❽ *Eisenstadt* → p. 75 to ❾ *Lake Neusiedl* → p. 72. Here you will experience a completely different aspect of Austria both in terms of the flat topography and Pannonian cultural influences. The ❿ *Neusiedler See/Seewinkel National Park* → p. 72, where even those who though that bird watching was a complete bore will discover just how fascinating it is, is a special highlight. This is followed by the greatest contrast imaginable: a visit to the metropolis of ⓫ *Vienna* → p. 75. The city has so much to offer that you should be sure to allow yourself enough time to discover all its charms: a visit to just a few of the main sights such as the Imperial Palace and St Stephan's Cathedral (photo right) will take several hours.

Experience the many facets of Austria
on this tour from Salzburg to Lake Neusiedl
and back again

PICTURE PERFECT

After you leave the imperial splendour of Vienna behind you, you continue on to the
⑫ *Wachau* → p. 71. The Danube cut a narrow valley in the hilly landscape between
⑬ *Krems* → p. 68 and ⑭ *Melk* → p. 70 that opens up unbelievable panoramic views.
The Wachau is not just nature; for centuries wine and apricots have been cultivated
here and the idyllic, well-fortified villages make it a complete work of art.

UNDER THE SIGN OF SALT

The Salzkammergut is the second to last destination on your journey. The old spa
town of ⑮ *Gmunden* → p. 49 is the gateway to this majestic landscape that was
carved by glaciers millenniums ago and
which was made wealthy by its salt de-
posits. On no account should you miss
out on visiting charming ⑯ *Bad Ischl*
→ p. 52, picturesque ⑰ *Hallstatt* → p. 52
and chic ⑱ *St Wolfgang* → p. 52.
Although you will find it difficult to tear
yourself away from this region, you
should pay attention to the time: the city
of ⑲ *Salzburg* → p. 56 is still waiting to
be explored. The Mozart City is the fitting
place to say your farewells to Austria.

1200 km (645mi)
Actual travel time 17 hrs
Recommended duration: a minimum
of at least two weeks. Detailed map of
the route on the back cover, in the road
atlas and the pull-out map

TYROL/ VORARLBERG

Mountains reign supreme in Tyrol. Only around 12% of the total area of the province (which is 4500mi²) can be used for agriculture. By way of comparison, the arable area is roughly the size of Greater London. Everything else is either forest or high alpine and glacier regions.

This makes it completely understandable that the third-largest province in Austria is also the most sparsely populated. Historical Tyrol is now divided into three sections: North Tyrol, with the capital city of Innsbruck, South Tyrol, which has been part of Italy since 1919 and East Tyrol, which remained with Austria but no longer has a common border with North Tyrol, with Lienz as its main city.

Wherever there are high mountains, there are deep valleys. In particular, there is guaranteed to be plenty of snow for skiing in winter in the Ötz, Stubai. Pitz and Samnaun Valleys south of the Inn Valley, and they are also magnificent summertime regions for hikers, mountain climbers and bikers. Holidaymakers looking for a more tranquil environment will find the valleys in East Tyrol especially attractive; the emphasis here is 'gentle tourism'.

After Vienna, Vorarlberg is the smallest province (1000mi²) in Austria and its cul-

Photo: Bregenz on Lake Constance, cable car on the Pfänder

Tyrol dominates with its high mountains and deep valleys, and Alemannic Vorarlberg displays a strong independent character

ture and language are quite different: Vorarlberg is part of the Alemannic linguistic and cultural area and, for this reason, wanted to join Switzerland after the monarchy collapsed, but the neighbouring country prevented it. In the east of the province, the Arlberg forms an important pass crossing as well as the border to Tyrol and – in the eyes of the Vorarlbergers – the rest of Austria.

BREGENZ

(136 A2) (*⌀ B5*) **The impressive location on Lake Constance (Bodensee) and the festival with the spectacular open-air stage on the lake make the city a hot spot in summer.**
In addition to the Kunsthaus, the extension to the Festival and Congress House

Modern cube of glass and steel: the Kunsthaus in Bregenz

is considered a successful example of functional, modern architecture. The settlement Brigantium was already fortified in the days of the Celts and was taken over and expanded by the Romans. Today, Bregenz with its 27,900 inhabitants is the second-smallest province capital.

SIGHTSEEING

KUNSTHAUS BREGENZ
The new symbol of Bregenz was designed by the Swiss architect Peter Zumthor and fascinates both inside and outside with its rational architecture that turns into a cube of light at night. Temporary exhibitions and a permanent collection of contemporary Austrian painting and sculpture including works by Kogler, Wurm and Zobernig. *Tue–Sun 10am–6pm, Thu 10am–9pm | entrance fee 9 euros | Karl-Tizian-Platz | www.kunsthaus-bregenz.at*

OBERSTADT WITH THE MARTIN TOWER ☼
Follow the cobblestone Maurachgasse and steep Stadtsteig until you reach the small, but very charming, 'upper city' that was established here by the Counts of Montfort in the years around 1250. The *ring wall,* built from the 13th to 16th centuries, is still largely preserved. You enter through the *Alte Stadttor (Old City Gate),* which is decorated with coats of arms. The mummified shark hanging in the archway is supposed to protect the city from harm. The main symbol of Bregenz is next to the city gate: the Baroque *Martin Tower* whose onion dome covered with wooden shingles is the largest in Central Europe. There is a splendid view from the tower and it also houses a *chapel* with notable Gothic frescoes that were most probably created by Swabian craftsmen in the 14th century *(April–Oct Tue–Sun 10am–5pm | entrance fee 3.50 euros | www.martinsturm.at).*

FOOD & DRINK

INSIDER TIP ▶ MAURACHBUND
Good, local cooking in pleasant surroundings; guest garden on the romantic terrace. *Daily | Maurachgasse 11 | tel. 05574 4 50 29 | www.maurachbund.com | Moderate*

NEUBECK

The creative, multi-cultural cuisine, which is not exactly inexpensive in the evening, served in this tastefully styled restaurant convinces sophisticated diners; there is also a reasonably priced lunchtime menu. The restaurant has a fairy-tale inner courtyard. *Closed Sun/Mon | Anton-Schneider-Str. 5 | tel. 05574 4 36 09 | www.neubeck. at | Moderate–Expensive*

SHOPPING

The various city markets sell regional products grown on nearby farms and other local specialities such as fish from Lake Constance: Sat at Leutbühel, Tue and Fri on Kornmarktstraße, Thu on Clemens-Holzmeister-Gasse and Fri on Kaiserstraße *(always in the morning)*. Fredis Käselädle is an award-winning cheese delicatessen shop *(Deuringstr. 9)*. There are also around 200 shops in the centre of the exhibition city Dornbirn around 13km (8mi) from Bregenz.

SPORTS & ACTIVITIES

Walkers, joggers, roller-bladers and cyclists will get their exercise on the shore of the lake where there is also a spacious modern *Strandbad (Strandweg 1)* waiting for those who want to go for a swim. The former INSIDER TIP Militärschwimmbad Mili (Military Baths; *Reichsstr., near the kiosk)*, a nostalgic building on wooden pillars, has a very special atmosphere. Hikers go up to the Pfänder where there are paths of all levels of difficulty from easy strolls to demanding tours. The *Pfänderbahn (daily 8am–7pm | ascent and descent 11.20 euros | Steinbruchgasse 4 | www.pfaenderbahn.at)* also transports hang-gliders and bicycles. Cyclists will enjoy the relaxed tours.

ENTERTAINMENT

During the festival season (in July and August every year) there is entertainment for all age groups and tastes on the lakeside promenade. The *s'Finanzamt* is a popular meeting place all year round *(daily | Brielgasse 21)* and the *Calypso (closed Mon/Tue | Bahnhofstr. 14)* a voguish discotheque.

WHERE TO STAY

BRIGANTIUM HOLIDAY ACCOMMODATION

Close to the centre but peaceful. The six flats are pleasantly furnished. *Merbodgasse 6–8 | tel. 0699 11 84 01 27 | www. tiscover.at/brigantium | Budget*

GOURMETHOTEL DEURING SCHLÖSSLE

The rooms and suites are all individually designed — with stucco ceilings and antiques or with sophisticated designer

---

⭐ **Bregenzerwald**
Magnificent forests and an El Dorado for cheese connoisseurs
→ p. 36

⭐ **Goldenes Dachl**
The symbol of Innsbruck has 2657 fire-gilded copper shingles
→ p. 38

⭐ **Bergisel Stadium**
An eye-catcher in two senses: ultramodern ski jump with a spectacular view of Innsbruck
→ p. 37

⭐ **Villgratental**
Unspoilt valley where rural life takes its course → p. 47

MARCO POLO HIGHLIGHTS

furniture. Exclusive hotel with equally exclusive cooking. *13 rooms | Ehre-Guta-Platz 4 | tel. 05574 4 78 00 | www.deuring-schloessle.at | Expensive*

INFORMATION

TOURIST INFORMATION
Rathausstr. 35 | 6900 Bregenz | tel. 05574 4 95 90 | tel. 05574 43 44 30 (room bookings) | www.bregenz.ws

WHERE TO GO

ARLBERG (136 C4) (*Ⓜ C6*)
The Arlberg pass crossing (1792m/5879ft) has a chequered history that reached its conclusion with the opening of the 14km (9mi)-long road tunnel in 1978. Arlberg is famous for its fashionable skiing areas and you will possibly even see royalty on the slopes around the towns of *Lech* and *Zürs*. Hiking and biking are very popular in summer. The leading hotel in the region is the *Gasthof Post (48 rooms | tel. 05583 2 20 60 | www.postlech.com | Expensive)* in Lech; 'guesthouse' is something of an understatement; VIPs from all around the world enjoy the laid-back 5-star comfort this establishment offers. *Around 90km (66mi) from Bregenz*

BREGENZERWALD (BREGENZ FOREST)
⭐ (136 B2–3) (*Ⓜ B–C5*)
This magnificent forest landscape, interspersed with pastures and meadows, retains a gentle appearance even though it has mountain peaks in excess of 2000m (6562ft). The wooden architecture that gives the villages a welcoming, warm character is typical for this area. The Bregenzerwald is made really special by the successful symbiosis of tradition, modern architecture – the time-honoured material of wood given new life through the use of glass – and cultural programmes, such as the *Schubertiade (www.schubertiade.at)* in Schwarzenberg

The dazzling colours make autumn especially beautiful in the Bregenz Forest

and Hohenems, being one of the most renowned series of events. Gourmets will explore the Bregenzerwald along the *Käsestraße (Cheese Route) (www.kaese strasse.at),* with visits to farming operations, tasting of the high-class products and entertaining events on the subject of cows and cheese. *www.bregenzerwald.at | around 30km (19mi) from Bregenz*

FELDKIRCH (136 A3) (*Ⓜ B6*)

The oldest city in the province is located on the border to Liechtenstein and enchants guests with its medieval character. The *Schattenburg* from the 12th century has a prominent position above the town and there is a row of patrician houses, churches and squares lined with arcades down below. *38 km (24mi) from Bregenz*

MONTAFON (136 B4) (*Ⓜ B6*)

The more than 30km (19mi)-long valley between Bludenz and Partenen, which is one of the largest hiking and skiing regions in the Alps, lies tucked away between the Silvretta group in the south, the Verwall in the north-east and Rätikon in the north-west. Numerous mountain railways whisk tourists up to the peaks – this makes it possible for them to avoid the strenuous ascent to the high mountain regions and they can set out on comparatively easy hikes; the view will take your breath away. There is a panoramic vista of the Piz Buin, with 3312m (10866ft) the highest mountain in Vorarlberg, from the ☀ Silvretta Reservoir, which can be reached over a 23km (14mi)-long mountain road. The ☺ *Explora Montafon (98 rooms | Gaschurn | tel. 05558 20 33 30 | www.explorer-hotel.com | Budget)* in Gaschurn promotes itself as a sports hotel. The budget, design hotel is the first certified passive house in Europe – it produces 90% less CO_2 than comparable hotels. *www. montafon.at | 60 km (37mi) from Bregenz*

WHERE TO START?
Get to the **Triumphal Arch** at the beginning of Maria-Theresien-Straße (for example, by tram 3, or city buses F, LK, R) and head north. You will soon reach the pedestrian precinct and enjoy the magnificent view of the Goldenes Dachl (Golden Roof) and the North Chain of the Alps rising up 2000m (6562ft) directly behind it.

INNSBRUCK

(138 A3) (*Ⓜ F6*) **Innsbruck was twice the site of Olympic Winter Games and the mountains have a tight hold on the city. Patscherkofel and the North Chain are part of the cityscape and the setting is made complete by the Karwendel Mountains in the north and Stubai and Tux Alps in the south.**

The noble town houses with their richly decorated façades, the peaceful arcades and narrow, winding streets in the pedestrian precinct around the Goldenes Dachl provide a fascinating contrast. Visitors soon realise that Italy is not far away. Innsbruck received its town charter around 1200 and has been Tyrol's capital city since 1849. Today, around 120,000 people live in this university and congress city; most of them work in service and hi-tech enterprises.

SIGHTSEEING

ALPENZOO (ALPINE ZOO) ● ☺

All of the 2000 animals that are kept in their natural environment originally had their habitat in the European Alpine region even though some of them, such as the bison and elk, no longer live there. The Alpenzoo has many successful rebreeding

Valley station of the Hungerburgbahn

and reintroduction projects. In addition, there is a model farm that is home to endangered working animals from the region. *Daily 9am–5pm, April–Oct to 6pm | entrance fee 8 euros | Weiherburggasse 37a | www.alpenzoo.at*

BERGISEL STADIUM ★ ⚜

The mountain achieved great historical importance as the main site of the Tyrolean struggle for freedom led by Andreas Hofer. Today, most people come to admire the spectacular ski jump and equally spectacular panoramic view. The tower, with an observation platform 250m (820ft) above the city offers a spectacular vista of Innsbruck, and is the centre of the newly built sporting complex designed by

the British architect Zaha Hadid. *Daily 10am–5pm, June–Oct 9am–6pm | entrance fee 9 euros | www.bergisel.info*

FERDINANDEUM

The Ferdinandeum provides an overview of all Tyrol has to offer in the areas of art and culture. Collections of objects from the prehistoric era and early history as well as the Roman period are complemented by admirable collections of works of classical and modern European art from Rembrandt to Wotruba. The late-Gothic collection is especially impressive. *Tue–Sun 9am–5pm | combi-ticket for all Tyrolean State Museums 10 euros | Museumstr. 15 | www.tiroler-landesmuseen. at. The other Tyrolean State Museums include the Court Church, the Museum of Folk Art and the Armoury.*

GOLDENES DACHL (GOLDEN ROOF) ★

Construction of what is probably the world's most famous oriel, which is covered with 2657 fire-gilded shingles, was completed in 1500. If you want to get a look inside the oriel, you will have to visit the *museum* devoted to Maximilian and the late-medieval period. *May–Sep daily 10am–5pm, Oct–April Tue–Sun 10am–5pm | entrance fee 4 euros | Herzog-Friedrich-Str. 15*

HOFKIRCHE (COURT CHURCH)

28 larger-than-life bronze statues – popularly called the *schwarze Mander* (black men) – stand guard over the cenotaph (empty grave) of Emperor Maximilian whose mortal remains are buried in Wiener Neustadt. The marble tombs in the wall niches of the *Silberne Kapelle (Silver Chapel)* are the final resting places of Archduke Ferdinand II and his first wife Philippine Welser. *Mon–Sat 9am–5pm, Sun 12.30–5pm | entrance fee 5 euros | Universitätsstr. 2*

HUNGERBURGBAHN ●

The ultramodern funicular, planned by Zaha Hadid, the architect who designed the tower on Bergisel, travels from the Congress Innsbruck station over Löwenhaus (Lion House) and Alpenzoo to the *Hungerberg* covering a distance of 1843m (6047ft) and a difference in altitude of 288m (945ft) on the way. You can imagine what the view is like after you change into the panorama gondolas of the Hafelekarbahn and finally reach an altitude of 2256m (7402ft)! Altogether, the trip from the city centre only takes about 20 minutes. *Daily | return ticket Hungerburgbahn 6.80 euros | return ticket Innsbruck–Hafelekar 27 euros | Rennweg 3 | www.nordkette.com*

AMBRAS CASTLE

Archduke Ferdinand II built this Renaissance castle on an exposed cliff on the edge of the city of Innsbruck. The highlights include the portrait gallery, the art and curiosity chambers, the armoury and the 43m (141ft)-long Spanish Hall. The INSIDERTIP▶ Mannerist chamber of curiosities, an encyclopaedic collection of all kinds of objects that brings together all of the knowledge of the period, is absolutely unique. The magnificent castle park is also well worth a visit. *Daily 10am–5pm, Aug until 6pm | entrance fee 10 euros, Dec–March 7 euros | Schlossstr. 20 | www.khm.at*

FOOD & DRINK

CAFÉ LICHTBLICK ⚘

The café on the 7th floor of the new town hall not only offers a splendid view of the Alps but also light cuisine and a pleasantly laid-back atmosphere. *Closed Sun | Maria-Theresien-Str. 18 | tel. 0512 56 65 50 | www.restaurant-lichtblick.at | Moderate*

LEWISCH

This inn has been open for 100 years and luckily you can still see this in its wood-panelled rooms. Down-to-earth Tyrolean specialities such as barley soup, dumplings and *gröstl*. *Daily, except on public holidays | Bienerstr. 19 | tel. 0512 58 60 43 | Budget*

VILLA BLANKA ⚘

This is where the up-and-coming generation of tourism experts is trained and the kitchen shows what it is capable of. The food – Tyrolean and international– is outstanding and the prices are unbelievable for this quality. The ambience is a bit austere but the view from the terrace of the spacious garden is unforgettable. *Closed Sun evening, Mon | Weiherburggasse 31 | tel. 0512 29 24 13 | www.villa-blanka.com | Moderate*

SHOPPING

Maria-Theresien-Straße is not only Innsbruck's most beautiful street with the best view; it is also the best place to go shopping. The *Kaufhaus Tyrol* is a classical department store with 100 years of tradition *(number 31)*; its modern counterpart is the elegant *Rathausgalerien* shopping mall *(number 18)*, with a 37m (121ft)- high glass campanile – sophisticated Innsbruckers are drawn to the brand-name stores, award-winning restaurant and design hotel. ☺ If you are looking for original Tyrolean souvenirs, you should head for the small shops in the neighbouring streets and in the old city such as the *Tiroler Bienenladen (Meraner Straße 2)* or *Tiroler Heimatwerk* at the same address. This is where you can buy biological herbal products, various kinds of *schnapps*, handicrafts, knitwear, table cloths and – of course – traditional clothing.

SPORTS & ACTIVITIES

Hafelekar and *Seegrube* offer a full programme and can be easily reached directly from the city: hiking, mountaineering, climbing and downhill-biking in summer and skiing, snowboarding and free riding in winter.

ENTERTAINMENT

Many students live in Innsbruck and this makes the city's nightlife lively, varied and comparatively inexpensive. There are venues for all tastes in the inner city including the in watering hole *Café-Bar Moustache (entrance: Badgasse)*, the cocktail, whisky, wine and champagne bar *Pfiffbar (Kaiserjägerstr. 2)* or the exclusive lounge *360-Grad-Bar (Rathausgalerien, Maria-Theresien-Straße 18)* with its spectacular view.

WHERE TO STAY

BINDERS

The hotel, which was built in the 1950s, has been beautifully renovated and a lot of attention paid to detail. Central location, quiet rooms on the courtyard side. *50 rooms | Dr.-Glatz-Str. 20 | tel. 0512 3 34 36 | www.binders.at | Budget*

THE PENZ

The design hotel is centrally located and has a cool bar and large ☼ terrace on the fifth floor where you can enjoy the spectacular view while eating your breakfast. *94 rooms | Adolf-Pichler-Platz 3 | tel. 0512 5 75 65 70 | www.thepenz.com | Expensive*

INFORMATION

INNSBRUCK TOURISMUS
Burggraben 3 | tel. 0512 5 98 50 | www.innsbruck.info

WHERE TO GO

ACHENSEE (138 A2) (∅ F5)
Tyrol's largest lake is at an altitude of 930m (3051ft) and is ideal for yachtsmen, surfers and kite-surfers. The glittering, emerald-green water is surrounded by the rugged Karwendel and multifaceted Rofan massif – the sports programme here includes hiking, mountain biking and climbing as well as paragliding. It is also possible to explore the lake leisurely by boat *(May–Oct | www.tirol-schiffahrt.at)* or electro-bike, which can now be hired and recharged in all villages. *www.achensee.info | around 42km (26mi) from Innsbruck*

NATIONAL HERO ANDREAS HOFER

Tyrol's official anthem, the 'Andreas Hofer Lied', begins with the words 'Loyal Hofer was taken in chains to Mantua/ In Mantua, the enemies led him to his death'. The freedom fighter Hofer was given a court martial and executed by a firing squad of French soldiers on 20 February 1810 in Mantua. He was the leader of the 1809 freedom movement against Bavaria's occupation by Napoleon. Although his peasant army had absolutely no chance against the French, Andreas Hofer is still considered a popular hero because he resisted until the very end. He was captured after being betrayed by one of his neighbours.

HALL (138 A3) (⌖ F6)

The 45m (148ft)-high Münzturm (Mint Tower), towers over this former salt-mining city, once a trading centre for salt and grain in the Middle Ages. Hall was granted the rights and privileges of a town back in 1303, although the absolutely harmonious ensemble of the old city could easily be considered a suburb of Innsbruck. The world's first large silver coin was minted here in 1486. The *Münze Hall (Hall Mint Museum) (Tue–Sun 10am–5pm, Nov, Dec, March, closed | combi-ticket Mint and Tower 8 euros | Burg Hasegg 6 | www. muenze-hall.at)* gives a presentation of Europe's minting history. Highlights include a unique roll embossing machine and the world's first thaler. It is worth climbing up the Gothic tower that also houses an exhibition. *11km (7mi) from Innsbruck*

ÖTZTAL (ÖTZ VALLEY)
(137 E3–5) (⌖ D–E 6–7)

The Ötztal is the longest tributary valley of the River Inn and provides a wealth of outstanding possibilities for hiking and biking. Rafting, canyoning, kayaking and canoeing are also offered at the entrance to the valley; several outdoor organisations such as *Feel Free* in Oetz *(www.feelfree. at)* arrange all kinds of wet action. Or, you can visit the new *Outdoor Area 47 (daily | Ötztal Station | www.area47.at)*, where your adrenalin rush will be increased with hi-tech on the gigantic water slides and other attractions. The Ötz Valley widens in the centre near Längefeld where hot sulphur springs bubble out of the earth. In the 16th century, there was a farmers' bath here but today you can relax in an ultramodern spa the *Aqua Dome (daily 9am–11pm | entrance fee for 3 hours 18 euros | www.aqua-dome.at)*. You can live with an ecologically clean conscience in the low-energy hotel the ☺ *Naturhotel Waldklause (50 rooms | Unterlängenfeld*

Mint Tower in Hall near Innsbruck

190 | tel. 05253 54 55 | www.waldklause. at | Expensive) that also fascinates with its unusual wood-glass-and-stone architecture. Everything revolves around skiing in the main town of Sölden (pop. 4100) at 1377m (4518ft) above sea level, from October to May. In 1991, headlines roared about the discovery of a mummified body of a young man who was discovered nearby on the Similaun glacier; *Ötzi* caused

The green giant spouts water for the Swarovski-Kristallwelten in Wattens

a furore in archaeological circles. You can get an impression of how life was lived around 5000 years ago in the Ötzidorf in Umhausen. *(May–Oct | Umhausen | www.oetzi-dorf.at). www.oetztal.com | around 50km (31mi) from Innsbruck*

SERFAUS (137 D4) (*ΩD6*)
The village facing south at an altitude of 1400m (4593ft) is blessed with a great deal of sunshine. 🕑 Cars were banned from the centre of the village so that they would not disturb anybody and there is an underground beneath the village street that can be used free of charge. Serfaus, as well as Ladis and Fiss, has a Rhaeto-Romanic past as is obvious from the façades of many farmhouses. Serfaus caters especially to families with children by providing special offers and services such as visiting the

marmots or 'prospecting for gold'. *(www.sommererlebniswelt.at)*. If you decide to stay at the 🕑 INSIDER TIP *Hotel Geiger (32 rooms | tel. 05476 62 66 | www.hotel-geiger.at | Untergasse 8 | Moderate)*, you will be able to choose between a Rhaeto-Romanic guesthouse and modern annex that has been conceived as a passive-energy house. *94km (58mi) from Innsbruck*

STUBAITAL (STUBAI VALLEY) (137 F4) (*ΩE6*)
The journey into the 35km (22mi)-long Stubai valley is lined with dolomite massifs and you will have a view of the glaciated end of the valley soon after you enter. This is an excellent region for carrying out all of the sports that are so typical in Tyrol: skiing in winter; hiking, mountaineering, climbing and biking in summer. The most

beautiful natural areas have been united under the name of *WildWaterPark (www.wildewasserweg.at);* signposts point the way to the thunderously raging – or peacefully gurgling – brooks, to waterfalls and springs. Mountaineers trek from hut to hut along the 120km (75mi) *Stubaier Höhenweg (Stubai Mountain Path);* those who want a less strenuous mountain experience can travel to the Kreuzjoch and, after a stop off at the ⛷ *observation platform*, let it all hang out on the wellness beds at the panorama lake *(www.schlick2000.at)*. The inquisitive can find out all about alpine plants on the *Alpenpflanzenpfad.* Cosy rooms are available in the *Cappella Natura Vitalis Hotel (26 rooms | Neustift | tel. 05226 25 15 | www.hotel-cappella.com | Moderate). www.stubai.com | 21 km (13mi) from Innsbruck*

WATTENS (138 A3) *(⌂ F6)*
The ● *Swarovski-Kristallwelten*, created by the multi-talented André Heller, are like a subterranean symphony composed of a magical world and curiosity cabinet, light and sound cathedrals, fairy-tales and fables. There is a shuttle bus to Wattens, 19km (12mi) away, four times a day from Innsbruck *(every 2 hours from 9am; from Main Station) (19.50 euros, free with the Innsbruck Card). Daily 9am–6.30 pm | entrance fee 11 euros | Kristallweltenstr. 1 | www.kristallwelten.com*

KITZBÜHEL

(138 C2) *(⌂ H5)* All ski fans know Kitzbühel (pop. 8200) as the site of the world-famous Hahnenkamm race.
The spruced-up little town between the Wilder Kaiser and Kitzbühel Alps looks good at any time of the year; it has become the home away from home for many stars and starlets. The Austrian skiing ace

Toni Sailer lived here until he died, as does Hansi Hinterseer, the one time wizard of the slopes who has now become a kind of modern troubadour with an enormous following in German-speaking countries, and football legend Franz Beckenbauer

MUSEUM KITZBÜHEL
The renovated and expanded museum shows the history of the town from mining in the bronze age to the 'skiing wonder' Toni Sailer. Some 30 paintings by the artist Alfons Walde (1891–1958), who lived in Kitzbühel, are displayed on the upper floor. *Dec–Easter Tue–Fri, Sun 2–6pm, Sat 10am–4pm, Easter–Oct Tue–Fri 10am–1pm, Sat 10am–5pm; in holiday periods, daily 10–5pm, Thu to 8pm | entrance fee 6 euros | Hinterstadt 32 | www.museum-kitzbuehel.at*

STREIF (THE STRIP)
The world's most difficult downhill course is on the Hahnenkamm: the *Streif*. If you follow the signs and hike here in summer, you will find it hard to believe that anybody would dare ski down it in winter – the so-called 'Mouse Trap' has an 85% gradient! You can reach the top with the *Hahnenkammbahn*, the 4.11km (2.55mi)-long hike begins at the *Starthaus*; the descent – an altitude difference of 900m (2853ft) – takes about two and a half hours; the *Seiflalm* is a good place to stop for refreshments.

CHIZZO
Cuisine, full of imagination, between down-to-earth and cosmopolitan, between Tyrolean and Mediterranean. *Daily | Josef-Herold-Str. 2 | tel. 05356 6 24 75 | www.chizzo.info | Moderate*

LOIS STERN

Modern, award-winning restaurant that attracts many VIPs where the food served not only tastes of the Alps but also of the rest of Europe and Asia. You can watch the chef Lois Stern at work in the large open kitchen. *Closed Sun, Mon | Josef-Pirchl-Straße 3 | tel. 05356 7 48 82 | Expensive*

SHOPPING

Sophisticated shopping in a pretty-as-a-picture village atmosphere – that is probably the best way to describe a shopping spree in Kitzbühel. The city centre boasts a number of haute-couture boutiques and designer shops, ranging from Boss, Louis Vuitton and Moncler to Bogner, Swarowski and Sportalm as well as some shops for first-class Tyrolean arts and crafts.

SPORTS & ACTIVITIES

Kitzbühel has something to satisfy almost every taste: 1000km (620mi) of hiking trails, 1200km (745mi) of racing-bike tracks, 800km (500mi) of routes for mountain biking, a total of 170 km (106mi) of ski slopes as well as walking and running tracks, four golf courses in the town alone, an indoor sports park, as well as the Schwarzsee with its 'healing' water invite holidaymakers to have the time of their lives. Kitzbühel is also increasingly focussing on e-bikes.

ENTERTAINMENT

The lights never really go out in Kitzbühel and the bars stay open until the early hours of the morning. VIPs from the film and sports world like to meet up in the *Beluna Bar (Hinterstadt 17)*, the bar in the *Hotel zur Tenne (Vorderstadt 8–10)* or go to the legendary *Take-Five (Hinterstadt 22)* to dance the night away.

WHERE TO STAY

BIOHOTEL FLORIAN ☺

The Pointner family offers first-class environmentally-friendly accommodation in nearby Reith: the electricity comes from clean sources; wood pellets and solar energy are used to produce the heating and warm water. Lovely, rustic rooms, organic food (vegetarian, whole-food diet), sunny meadow location. *32 rooms | Bichlach 41 | Reith bei Kitzbühel (6 km/4mi) | tel. 05356 6 52 42 | www.hotel-florian.at | Moderate*

HOTEL ZUR TENNE

This is where the action is; there might be an aristocrat or one of the rich and powerful in the room next to yours if you stay in this traditional, elegant hotel; fireplace, whirlpool or steam bath in the rooms. *51 rooms | Vorderstadt 8–10 | tel. 05356 64 44 40 | www.hotelzurtenne.com | Expensive*

INFORMATION

KITZBÜHEL TOURISMUS
Hinterstadt 18 | tel. 05356 6 66 60 | www. kitzbuehel.com

WHERE TO GO

KUFSTEIN (138 C2) *(Ⓜ G5)*

If you drive into Tyrol over the Inntal Auto-bahn, you will see the ✲ *Festung Kufstein (Kufstein Fortress) (April–Oct daily 9am–5pm, Nov–March 10am–4pm | entrance fee 9.90 euros)* from afar standing proudly above the town (pop. 17,400). The roots of the impressive fortress can be traced back to the year 1205. It covers an area of 280,000ft² making it larger than the old town of Kufstein, which is also well worth a visit and is often the venue of major events. There is an especially fascinating view over the town and the Inn Valley. The world's largest open-air organ

The Kufstein Fortress stands proudly above the town of the same name

with 46 registers and 4307 pipes is played every day at noon. The motto of the modern glassworks which can be visited at *Riedel Glas (Mon–Fri | entrance fee 5 euros | www.riedel.com)* is SINNfonie. *www.kufstein.com | 37km (23mi) from Kitzbühel*

ZILLERTAL (ZILLER VALLEY)
(138 B3–4) *(ⒷⒷ F–G6)*
The 30km (19mi)-long valley is the epitome of holidays in Tyrol with its picturesque villages where traditions are kept alive, green meadows and gently rising mountain slopes that narrow at the end to form four alpine valleys. Drivers who have no fear of mountains will be enthusiastic about the *Zillertaler Höhenstraße* with its corresponding uphill stretches and fantastic views. The ☺ *Hochgebirgs-Naturpark Zillertaler Alpen (Ziller Valley Alpine Nature Park)* has been established in the far south; at an altitude of 1000 to 3500m (3250 to 11,500ft), it covers all of the levels of the Central Alps. It offers an exceptional variety of fauna and flora, as well as more

than 80 glaciers and many mountain and cirque lakes. Hikes on special subjects are organised in summer *(www.naturpark-zillertal.at)*. The Ziller Valley is also renowned for the respect the people living there pay to their age-old customs as seen in the many festivities held throughout the year. However, sometimes tradition and the new generation rub shoulders: the Ziller Valley is famous throughout Europe as a hot party zone for folksy music.

LIENZ

(139 D5) *(ⒷⒷ H7)* **The capital city (pop. 12,000) of East Tyrol is located at the confluence of the Drau and Isel rivers and is a real 'gem in a predominantly mountainous and densely forested region'.**
This comment made by a 15th-century visitor to Lienz is still valid today. The main square is lined with distinguished town houses and exudes charm and hospitality at any time of the year.

SIGHTSEEING

MUSEUM DER STADT LIENZ
Cultural and art-historical treasures, as well as important works by Albin Egger-Lienz are on display in Schloss Bruck. *Mid-May–mid-Sept daily 10am–6pm, mid-Sept–mid-Oct Tue–Sun 10am–4pm | entrance fee 7.50 euros | Schlossberg 1 | www.museum-schlossbruck.at*

FOOD & DRINK

FALKENSTEIN
Brewery restaurant on the road towards Sillian with home-brewed beer and regional cooking. *Daily | Pustertaler Str. 40 | tel. 04852 6 22 70 | Budget–Moderate*

LOW BUDGET

▶ In summer, Kitzbühel Tourismus organises ● free hikes on weekdays *(Mon–Fri)*. The two guides Engelbert and Madeleine place great value on showing their guests the loveliest spots near the small town. The hikes take place from mid-May to the end of October and there are two hikes organised to cater for the different levels of proficiency during the peak summer period from mid-June to mid-September.

▶ In the ● *Bregenzerwälder Käsekeller* you will be able to buy the best mountain cheese at unbeatable prices: the cheese, at different degrees of maturity, comes straight to the shop from the Alpine dairy farms and is made from silo-free milk. *Mon–Fri 10am–6pm, Sat 9am–5pm | Zeihenbühel 423 | Lingenau | www.kaesekeller.at*

SPORTS & ACTIVITIES

Lienz is surrounded by wonderful hiking paths, cycle and mountain-bike tracks which cater to all levels of proficiency *(Bike-Arena Lienzer Dolomiten)*. Those who enjoy white-water sports will find just what they are looking for: rafting, canoeing, kayaking and canyoning. Information: *Outdoor Camp Osttirol | Ainet | tel. 0664 3 56 04 50 | www.osttirol-adventures.at*

WHERE TO STAY

GRIBELEHOF
Traditional guesthouse on the Schlossberg, with the most spectacular view over Lienz. *16 rooms | Schlossberg 9 | tel. 04852 6 21 91 | www.gribelehof.com | Moderate*

INFORMATION

OSTTIROL WERBUNG
Albin-Egger-Str. 17 | tel. 050 21 22 12 | www.osttirol.com

WHERE TO GO

AGUNTUM (139 D–E5) (*∅ J7*)
The Roman excavations bear witness to a settlement from early antiquity that was razed to the ground by the Huns in the 5th century and started to be unearthed in the 18th century. The *Archäologische Museum* shows finds discovered there *(June–mid-Sep daily 9.30am–6pm, mid-Sept–Oct 9.30am–4pm, May Mon–Sat 9.30am–4pm | entrance fee 6 euros, combi-ticket with Schloss Bruck 10.50 euros)*. 4km (2.5mi) from Lienz

KALS (139 D4) (*∅ H7*)
The old wooden houses in this small village at the foot of the Großglockner make it a model mountain settlement. Specialities from the *Hohe Tauern National Park* re-

The outlines of the Roman settlement Aguntum become clear from the platform

gion are sold in 🙂 crafts shops. The most spectacular view of the Großglockner is from the ⚶ INSIDER TIP car park at the *Lucknerhaus* (1918m/6293ft), which can be reached via the alpine road from Kals into the Ködnitz Valley *(8 euros toll per car / 7km/4.5mi)*. This is not only the starting point for hikes in the mountains or from hut to hut, but also for the *Themenlehrpfad Glocknerspur (Glockner Educational Trail)* lasting around one hour. *32km (20mi) from Lienz*

UMBAL WATERFALLS (138 C4) *(ⓜ G7)*
In hardly any other valley in the Hohe Tauern Mountains are the effects that a glacier brook can have on shaping the landscape as visible as they are from the *Wasserschaupfad (Water Observation Path)*, from which you can observe the spectacular stepped falls of the Isel River. It is about half an hour from the Ströden car park. The walk along the path takes from one to two hours and there is a difference in altitude of around 130m (427ft). *45 km (28mi) from Lienz*

VILLGRATENTAL ★ 🙂
(138 C5) *(ⓜ G–H7)*
Villgraten Valley is an idyll straight out of a picture book: pure country life, untouched by the outside world. It starts in *Außervillgraten* and, after many curves, leads you to picturesque *Innervillgraten,* shortly thereafter charming *Kalkstein,* and then ends abruptly in the mountains. There are no lifts in the Villgraten Valley although there is no lack of snow-covered slopes. Go for a hike, collect mushrooms and then just lay back and relax. The farmhouses of the INSIDER TIP *Gannerhof (24 rooms / Innervillgraten | tel. 04843 52 40 | www. gannerhof.at | Expensive)* are as old as the hills and are the perfect place to spend the night in harmony with the region. You will feel right at home and the cooking is sensational. The resourceful Schett family's life revolves around their sheep, but they are always happy to welcome guests to their *Haus Villgrater Natur (Mon–Fri 7.30am–noon, 1.30–6pm, Sat 9am–noon; in summer, to 5pm | www.villgraternatur. at)*. *40 km (25mi) from Lienz*

UPPER AUSTRIA/ SALZBURG

The Salzkammergut in the heart of Austria unites the most beautiful sections of the provinces of Upper Austria, Styria and Salzburg. Salt mining made the area wealthy and the industry still continues in Bad Ischl, Altausee and in the the oldest salt mine of all, Hallstatt.

Today, city dwellers in search of recreation and those who love the water are attracted to the shores of the clear lakes. This is the ideal region for a traditional summer holiday. The province of Salzburg, with the world-famous Mozart city as its capital, is divided into five districts: Pinzgau, Pongau, Lungau, Tennengau and Flachgau. However, the division of the province into the *inner Gebirg* (inner mountains) and flat remainder – the German word for flat *flach* in Flachgau describes the topography – is more significant. The 3000 metre (10,000ft)-peaks of the Hohe Tauern Mountains, including the Großglockner and Großvenediger, set the scene in the 'inner mountains' and provide excellent conditions for skiing in winter and hiking and mountaineering in summer. The landscape around the city of Salzburg is inviting and made even more pleasant by the lovely lakes and mild climate.

Most of Upper Austria's landscape spreads out to the north of the main ridge of the Alps and is dominated by the Bohemian

Crystal-clear lakes and Mozart's home town: the special fascination of this region lies in the interplay between culture and nature

Massif in the Mühlviertel. The fourth largest Austrian province is divided into four regions or quarters: the Mühlviertel (Mill Quarter) in the north, the Inn- and Hausruckviertel (named after the River Inn and Hausruck range of hills) in the west and the Traunviertel (Traun River Quarter) that stretches from the south to the west. The highest mountain in the Upper Austrian Alps is the Dachstein with an altitude of 2995m (9826ft). The youthful, vital province capital Linz was European Capital of Culture in the year 2009.

GMUNDEN

(132 C5) (*ℳ L4*) This city (pop. 13,100), with its picturesque location at an altitude of 422m (1385ft) on the northern shore

Orth Castle – a medieval gem on Lake Traun

of Lake Traun, has trading in salt to thank for its importance. Gmunden is also well-known for its ceramics factory.

Today, the spa city's main drawing card is its beautiful site on the lake surrounded by mountains. The Esplanade invites Gmunden's guests to take a stroll on balmy summer evenings.

SIGHTSEEING

KAMMERHOF MUSEUM

A modern museum in the former salt office deals with different topics in its 14 rooms; however, the red thread running through the collection is the material of ceramics. The exhibition of sanitary equipment 'Klo & So' is especially offbeat. *June–Aug Tue–Sun, Sept–May Wed–Sun 10am–5pm | entrance fee 6 euros | Kammerhofgasse 8 | www.museen.gmunden.at*

SCHLOSS ORTH

The eleventh-century castle on a small island in the lake, is considered the symbol of the Upper Austrian Salzkammergut. It is actually not a hotel but a popular place for weddings with its registry office, chapel and landing place for ships.

FOOD & DRINK

KONDITOREI-CAFÉ GRELLINGER

You must try the *Gmundner Torte* (shortcrust pastry with nuts) in this famous pastry shop. *Sept–June, closed Wed | Franz-Joseph-Platz 6 | tel. 07612 6 41 53*

RESTAURANT ORTHER STUB'N

There is also a restaurant in the castle on the lake where one guests can enjoy freshly caught fish and regional specialities. *Daily, closed in Feb, Oct–end of April closed Mon | tel. 07612 6 24 99 | www.schlossorth. com | Moderate*

SHOPPING

For 300 years now, each piece produced by the ceramic factory ☺ Gmundner Keramik Manufaktur has been painted by hand. Guided tours by appointment. *Keramikstr. 24 | Mon–Sat, April–Oct also on Sun | www.gmundner-keramik.at*

SPORTS & ACTIVITIES

Lake Traun offers everything water sports fans desire, provided they are not sensitive about the temperature: sailing, surfing, kiting, water skiing and wake-boarding, diving and kayaking. And, of course, Gmunden is also a good spot for hiking and mountain biking. Hang-gliders and paragliders love the 1594m (5230ft)-high Feuerkogel near Ebensee. The other lakes in the Salzkammergut also provide a great variety of options: you can choose between golfing and road biking (Lake Fuschl region), trekking (Dachstein) and fishing. www.salzkammergut.at

WHERE TO STAY

HOIS'N WIRT
The Schallmeiner family has provided guests with a summer idyll for more than 100 years; on the outskirts of the town, this traditional hotel has its own private beach and exceptionally good food. *44 rooms | Traunsteinstr. 277 | tel. 07612 7 73 33 | www.hoisnwirt.at | Moderate*

INFORMATION

FERIENREGION TRAUNSEE/ TOURISMUSBÜRO GMUNDEN
Am Rathausplatz 1 | 4810 Gmunden | tel. 07612 65 75 2 | www.traunsee.at

WHERE TO GO

ATTERSEE (LAKE ATTER)
(132 B–C 5–6) (ΜΠ K4)
Attersee, the 'Linzers' Ocean', is Austria's largest inland lake and a popular bathing destination. The most impressive view of the majestic backdrop of the Höllengebirge is from the lake. *Unterach* is famous for its stilt houses that bear witness to its early settlement and *Steinbach* attracts music lovers to the small hut where Gustav Mahler composed during the several summers he spent here. You will enjoy the imperial flair of dining in the INSIDER TIP *Kaisergasthof (daily, Oct–May closed Mon/Tue | Weyregger Str. 75 | Weyregg | tel. 07664 22 02 | www.kaisergasthof.at | Moderate)* with classic dishes such as soup with savoury sponge, old-Viennese style boiled beef and apple strudel. There is also a small *Habsburg Museum* on the premises. *31km (19mi) from Gmunden*

BAD ISCHL (132 C6) (*m K4*)

The spa and operetta town (pop. 14,000) still lives from the flair of the imperial days of the past. The former *Emperor's Villa (April–Oct daily, Jan–March Wed 10am– 4pm | entrance fee 12.50 euros | www. kaiservilla.com)*, which is full of memories of Franz Joseph and his wife Sisi, is still the home of Markus Habsburg, a great grandson of the emperor. The *Konditorei Zauner* is a legendary pastry shop; in summer, the guests sit directly on the Traunesplanade and enjoy the shop's speciality the INSIDER TIP *Zaunerstollen* that is made using a secret recipe. The *Eurotherme (www.eurothermen.at)* is a fine place to relax. Guests can dine in style and relatively inexpensively in the ● *Weinhaus Attwenger (closed Mon, mid-Sept–April closed Mon, Tue | Leharkai 12 | www. attwenger-weinhaus.at | Moderate)*, a historical salt merchant's house with a fairy-tale garden on the bank of the River Traun. *35km (22mi) from Gmunden*

HALLSTATT ★ (140 A1) (*m K5*)

According to Alexander von Humboldt, Hallstatt (pop. 815), with its idyllic location between the lake and towering steep rock face, is the 'the world's most beautiful lake village'. Hallstatt is also important in the field of art history: the burial ground above the village gave an entire ice-age epoch its name. The ● *salt mine* next to it has been in operation for more than 3500 years *(tours of the mine | www.salz welten.at)*. Hallstatt is in the heart of the Unesco World Heritage site Inneres Salzkammergut/Dachstein. The pleasant INSIDER TIP *Bräugasthof (Seestr. 120 | tel. 06134 82 21 | www.brauhaus-lobisser.com | Moderate)* serves fish fresh from the lake and is also a splendid place to spend the night. You should definitely plan to visit the Dachstein Massif (cable-car station in nearby Obertraun), where you can explore

gigantic caves, put your fear of heights to the test at the spectacular observation platform on the ☃ *Krippenstein* called the '5 Fingers' with five footbridges over a 400m vertical drop, and/or spend a day hiking. If you decide to stay on the lakeside, you will have a magnificent view across the lake to Hallstatt from the ● *Strandbad* in Obertraun. *54km (34mi) from Gmunden*

ST WOLFGANG (132 B6) (*m K4*)

What was once an important place of pilgrimage became famous overnight when Ralph Benatzky's operetta 'The White Horse Inn' was premiered in 1930. The Gothic Pacher Alter in the parish church from the 12th century is well worth seeing. The ☃ *Schafberg* can be reached by a rack railway and there is a spectacular view over the Salzkammergut from the top. The laid-back *Leopoldhof (14 rooms | Ried 8 | tel. 06138 24 38 | www.leopoldhof.at | Budget)* has its own beach and a spacious sunbathing lawn directly by the lake. *50 km (31mi) from Gmunden*

LINZ

(133 D–E4) (*m M3*) **The Main Square (Hauptplatz) of the Upper Austrian capital (pop. 192,000) is lined with Baroque**

> **CITY** **WHERE TO START?**
> Take the tram (line 1, 2 or 3) and start the day on the top floor of the **Ars Electronica Center** with the city spread out at your feet. No matter whether you intend to continue your city trip with a visit of the Center, the Lentos Art Museum, the Castle Museum, the Main Square or Postlingberg: they are all just a short walk away.

The marble Trinity Column on the main square in Linz is 20m (66ft) high

façades and there is a magnificent Trinity Column (1723) in its middle.

However, although this is one of the largest built-up squares in Europe, Linz's main attraction lies in its history as an industrial city and its most recent past as a cultural metropolis: Linz was the European Capital of Culture in the year 2009.

SIGHTSEEING

ALTER DOM (OLD CATHEDRAL)

The Ignatius Church, which is known as the Old Cathedral, was once the bishop's church where Anton Bruckner served as an organist for more than ten years. It is an impressive building in the Italian Baroque style (17th century) *Domgasse 3*

ARS ELECTRONICA CENTER ★ ●

Bio- and genetic-technology, neurology, robotics, prosthetics, and media art amalgamate in interactive installations to form pioneering experimental arrangements, in which those things that will possibly

determine our lives in the future can be put to the test. The brightly illuminated animation façade at night is particularly attractive. *Tue–Fri 9am–5pm (Thu to 9pm), Sat/Sun 10am–6pm | entrance fee 8 euros | Ars-Electronica-Str. 1 | www.aec.at*

LENTOS ART MUSEUM

The Museum with its severe glass-and-concrete exterior on the banks of the Danube houses a considerable collection of classical modern art with works by Klimt, Schiele, Kokoschka and Pechstein as well as contemporary art with paintings by Lassnig, Rainer, Lüpertz and many others. In addition, there are temporary exhibitions of the most recent forms of international art. *Tue–Sun 10am–6pm (Thu to 9pm) | entrance fee 6.50 euros | Ernst-Koref-Promenade 1 | www.lentos.at*

PÖSTLINGBERG ☼

The densely wooded Postlingberg with its prominent pilgrimage basilica stands proudly above the city. The historical track

Shopping arcade on Linzer Landstraße

VOEST-ALPINE STAHLWELT

This exhibition and tour of the works will make it possible for you to get a behind-the-scenes view of how steel is produced and acquaint you with the latest technologies in the field. *Exhibition: Mon–Sat 9am–5pm | 8 euros | works tour: Tue–Fri by appointment, Sat 10.30am and 2pm | 8 euros | Voest-Alpine-Str. 4 | www.voest alpine-stahlwelt.at*

FOOD & DRINK

FREISEDER ☺

Traditional country pub on the Pöstling-berg. Large selection of good plain food and Viennese cuisine; home-made apple juice and cider. *Closed Mon/Tue | Freiseder-weg 2 (can be reached by the Pöstlingberg railway) | tel. 0732 73 15 60 | Budget*

P'AA ☺

Great restaurant for vegetarians, vegans and all those who attach great importance to biologically controlled products. *Closed Sat/Sun | Altstadt 28 | tel. 0732 77 64 61 | www.paa.cx | Moderate*

VERDI

This is the place to experience great regional and Italian flavours and the way the food is served is also a feast for the eyes. Chef Erich Lukas insists on only using freshly harvested products. The panorama terrace is an especially pleasant place to sit and have your dinner. *Tue–Sat from 5pm | Pachmayrstr. 137 | tel. 0732 73 30 05 | www.verdi.at | Expensive*

SHOPPING

Landstraße, the road from the train station to the main square, is the city's main shopping strip with large shops and covered arcades; the smaller speciality shops and boutiques can be found in the side streets.

mountain railway, the steepest on the continent, transports visitors directly from Linz's main square in just 20 minutes – if you are interested, you can get off at the middle station and visit the Linz Zoo. *Mon–Sat 6am–10pm, Sun from 7.30am, every half-hour | return ticket 6.50 euros | Hauptplatz*

SCHLOSSMUSEUM LINZ ☆

The Castle Museum is the largest universal museum in Austria. With permanent exhibitions on nature and technology as well as temporary shows. Unforgettable: the view across the roofs of the city from the terrace. *Tue–Fri 9am–6pm, Thu to 9pm, Sat/Sun 10am–5pm | entrance fee 6.50 euros | Schlossberg 1 | www.landes museum.at*

A *Linzer Torte* (a cake with current or raspberry jam) makes an original souvenir; the Bäckerei *Hoffmann (Landstr. 27)* packs them very attractively. A ☺ *farmers' market* is held every Friday *(10am–2pm)* on the main square in Linz – this is also the location of the *flea market* on Saturday *(7am–2pm)*.

ENTERTAINMENT

The night-time hot spots, such as the hip *Vanilli (Hofgasse 8)* or the *Easy (Baumbachstr. 14)* cocktail bar, are all located within easy walking distance of each other each other in the centre of town. The *Posthof (Posthofstr. 43 | www.posthof. at)* is *the* place to go in Linz for way-out, alternative entertainment.

WHERE TO STAY

DOMHOTEL
The colours of the interior, light blue, white and beige, were carefully chosen to create a feeling of relaxation. ☺ The furniture was produced by local carpenters. *40 rooms | Baumbachstraße 17 | tel. 0732 77 84 41 | www.cityhotel.at | Moderate*

INSIDER TIP ▶ PIXELHOTEL
The individual rooms and suites are scattered throughout the city: in an old shop, in a backyard workshop or on a ship – they have all been superbly renovated and are absolutely tip-top. Guests have to go to one of the nearby coffee houses for their breakfast. *5 rooms | tel. 0650 7 43 79 53 | www.pixelhotel.at | Moderate*

INFORMATION

TOURIST INFORMATION
Hauptplatz 1 | Tel. 0732 70 70 20 09 | www. linz.at

WHERE TO GO

BÖHMERWALD (BOHEMIAN FOREST)
(132–133 C–D2) *(ᗰ L1–2)*
The gentle contours of the Bohemian Forest lend a very distinctive character to the border area between the Czech Republic and Bavaria. The region is an ideal place to get away from the stress of everyday life and go hiking – along the Schwarzenberg Canal for example or to the neighbours across the border at the Moldau River reservoir. This is also the perfect area for skiing excursions with the entire family in winter *(Hochficht)*, a INSIDER TIP ▶ fabulous centre for Nordic sports *(Schöneben)* and it is even possible to go dog sledding *(Aigen)*. *www.boehmerwald.at | 55 km (34mi) from Linz*

STEYR (133 E5) *(ᗰ M3)*
The historical core of Steyr is located on a peninsula at the confluence of the Rivers Steyr and Enns. It is easy to recognise how this city, which was a main centre of iron

LOW BUDGET

▶ You can bathe in comfort and free of charge in Lake Hallstatt at the *Seebad Obertraun*. Old trees provide shade and, from here, you have a fine view of the turquoise-coloured lake of Hallstatt in the distance.

▶ If you have several palaces, castles and museums on your itinerary, you should definitely buy the *Salzburg Card (25/34/40 euros of 24/48/72 hours)*. This enables you to visit all of the major attractions in the city and use the public transport system without paying any extra within the specified period.

production, increased in prosperity over the centuries. The cityscape is dominated by splendid town houses from the Gothic to Rococo periods; the town hall is a particularly beautiful example. Steyr is still the home of important industrial enterprises. *43km (27mi) from Linz*

ST FLORIAN ★ (133 E4) (*𝄞 M3*)

This monastery of the Augustine canons was founded in 1071 and is one of the most impressive religious houses in Austria. The heart of the complex is formed by the two-towered abbey church, completed by Jakob Prandtauer, the library wing and the marble hall with frescoes by Altomonte. The composer Anton Bruckner had close ties with the monastery where he was a choir boy and later organist. *Guided tours May–Sept daily 11am, 1 and 3pm | 7.50 euros | organ concerts mid-May–mid-Oct daily except Tue and Sat at 2.30pm | entrance fee 4 Euro, combi-ticket with guided tour 9 euros. 20km (12mi) from Linz*

SALZBURG

(132 A6) (*𝄞 J4*) **Salzburg (pop. 148,000), Mozart's birthplace and Unesco World Heritage Site, is synonymous for majestic churches, magnificent palaces, narrow streets and peaceful corners.**

The view from the fortress or the terrace of the Museum der Moderne (Museum of Modern Art) reveals just how beautiful this city and its surroundings are. Salt gave the region and the city their names. Christian missionaries settled where Celts and Romans once had their places of worship. The prince-archbishops, especially Wolf Dietrich von Raitenau who was implemental in giving Salzburg its Baroque appearance, made the city what it is today.

SIGHTSEEING

ALTE RESIDENZ

The origins of the centre of power of the prince-archbishops date back to the 12th century; the appearance of the residence today is the result of work carried out between the late 16th and 18th centuries. *Daily 10am–5pm | entrance fee 9 euros | Residenzplatz 1*

CATHEDRAL

The early Baroque building planned by Santino Solari has room for more than 10,000 worshippers. The bright interior, further emphasised by the 75m (246ft)-high cupola, is especially notable. The façade with its two towers provides the impressive setting for performances of 'Everyman' during the festival in the summer. *Residenzplatz/Kapitelplatz*

HOHENSALZBURG FORTRESS ★

It stands proudly above the town on a 199m (653ft)-high dolomite massif and is one of the largest castle complexes in Central Europe. The Golden Room, Golden Hall and Fortress Church, can only be visited as part of a guided tour. *May–Sept daily 9am–7pm, Oct–April 9am–5pm | entrance fee 7.80 euros, 11 euros with cable car | www.salzburg-burgen.at*

> **CITY** **WHERE TO START?**
> The funicular railway on Festungsgasse (bus station: Mozartsteg-Rudolkskai, with lines 3, 5 or 6; there is a car park on Franz Josef Kai) takes visitors up to the **Hohensalzburg Fortress**. The unforgettable view over the narrow streets of the Mozart city provides the first orientation. Take the railway back down and you will find yourself again in the midst of the hustle and bustle of the city.

Wolfgang Amadeus Mozart was born at Getreidegasse 9 in 1756

MIRABELL

Wolf Dietrich erected this palace for Salome Alt, the mother of his 14 children, in 1606. The garden was laid out following plans drawn up by Johann Bernhard Fischer von Erlach. The Marble Hall is a popular place for weddings during the day and concerts at night. *Marble Hall Mon, Wed, Thus 8am–4pm, Tue, Fri 1–4pm, Mirabellgarten 6am to nightfall | free admission*

MOZART'S BIRTHPLACE ★

The yellow-painted house on Getreidegasse is a place of pilgrimage for admirers of Mozart. This is where Wolfgang Amadeus was born on 27 January 1756. Original instruments, including the violin Mozart played as a child and his clavichord, furniture, paintings and facsimiles of letters are on display in the family's former apartment. *Sept–June daily 9am–5.30pm, July/Aug 9am–8pm | entrance fee 7 euros | Getreidegasse 9*

MUSEUM DER MODERNE

Thematic and monographic exhibitions of 20th and 21st century art are shown at two locations: in the Baroque Rupertinum in the heart of the old city and the spectacular new building on the Mönchsberg high above the city roofs; the architecture alone makes it worth a visit. *Tue–Sun 10am–6pm, Wed to 8pm | combi-ticket for both venues 12 euros | Wiener Philharmoniker Gasse 9 and Mönchsberg 32 | www.museumdermoderne.at*

SALZBURG MUSEUM NEUE RESIDENZ

Wolf Dietrich's former palace for his guests is located on the west side of the Residenzplatz. The permanent exhibition in the state rooms on the second floor concentrates on Salzburg's development in history, art and culture since the beginning of the modern age. *Tue–Sun 9am–5pm | entrance fee 7 euros | Mozartplatz 1 | www.salzburgmuseum.at*

Roman theatre with fountains in Hellbrunn Castle

SCHLOSS HELLBRUNN

Prince-Archbishop Markus Sittikus von Hohenems, who was a great admirer of Italian art and culture, commissioned the architect of the Salzburg Cathedral, Santino Solari, with work on this building in 1612. Water is the main element in the layout: hidden in the shade of trees and bushes or shooting out of unexpected hiding places – the fountains and waterworks are the world-famous heart of this castle. *Daily 9am–4.30pm, May/June, Sept to 5.30pm, July/Aug to 9pm | entrance fee 9.50 euros | www.hellbrunn.at*

FOOD & DRINK

CARPE DIEM FINEST FINGERFOOD

Highly-praised, trendy fusion restaurant devoted to creative fingerfood – the ideal place to take a break from shopping and sit on the terrace in the centre of Getreidegasse. Large gourmet restaurant on the 1st floor. *Fingerfood daily 8.30am–midnight, Restaurant closed Sun | Getreidegasse 50 | tel. 0662 84 88 00 | www.carpe diemfinestfingerfood.com | Moderate–Expensive*

INSIDER TIP GÖSSL GWANDHAUS

The Gössl Gwandhaus is actually a tailor's shop for traditional apparel. But the castle atmosphere is so splendid that a beautiful restaurant also opened here in 2011. Exquisite regional cuisine; reasonably priced set meals at lunchtime. *Daily | Morzger Straße 31 | tel. 0662 46 96 60 | www.gwandhaus.com | Moderate*

PAULI STUBM

This inn, with its charming little beer garden in the inner city, has achieved cult status. Simple cooking (*Kasnock'n*/cheese gnocchi, *Knödel*/dumplings, *Ofenkartoffel*/baked potatoes, *Schweinsbraten*/roast pork) in very attractive surroundings. *Mon–Sat from 5pm | Herrengasse 16 | tel. 0662 84 32 20 | www.paul-stube.at | Budget*

SHOPPING

Many traditional manufacturers, from liqueur makers to confectioners, have their address in the romantic inner courtyards around Getreidegasse. The *Mora Bookshop* on Residenzplatz, the *Alte fürsterzbischöfliche Hofapotheke* (Old Prince-Archbishop Court Chemists) on Alter Markt, the *Holzermayr Chocolate Manufacture*, the *St Peter Monastery Bakery*, *Anton Koppenwallner's goldsmith atelier* and the *Schatz pastry shop* are just some of the time-honoured establishments. However, you should be sure that you have plenty of money with you when you set out on a shopping spree here – Salzburg is an expensive spot. Admirers of traditional clothing will be well taken care of in the *Gössl Gwandhaus* (see Food & Drink, p. 24).

ENTERTAINMENT

The rooftop terrace of the *Hotel Stein* near the Staatsbrücke is a pleasant place to start the evening. On this side of the Salzach River, you can make your way either along picturesque Steingasse where there is a string of bars and inns – from the *Shrimpsbar* and *Saitensprung Club* to the *Andi Hofer Beisl* – or Giselakai. The nightlife here is especially chic in *Chez Roland* or the *Living Room Bazillus*. Irish pubs and American bars set the scene across the river on Rudolfskai; if you head off towards the Mönchsberg, you will come across some of long-established Salzburg nightlife institutions such as the *republic (Anton-Neumayr-Platz)* or *Flip (Gstättengasse)*.

WHERE TO STAY

INSIDER TIP ALL YOU NEED HOTEL SALZBURG

This comfortable hotel at the foot of the Kapuzinerberg satisfies its guests with reasonable prices in spite of its location near the town centre. *69 rooms | Glockengasse 4 b | tel. 050 11 43 | www.allyouneed hotels.at | Budget*

BLAUE GANS

Trendy art hotel in historical vaults vis-à-vis the Festspielhaus. Cool rooms, popular bar, top-class restaurant. *40 rooms | Getreidegasse 41–43 | tel. 0662 84 24 91 50 | www.blauegans.at | Expensive*

HOTEL ZUR POST ☺

This family-run hotel in a central location has been granted the Austrian Environment Award. A lot of the fittings in the room are made of local wood; the products on the breakfast table come from organic farms. *Maxglaner Hauptstr. 45 | tel. 0662 8 38 23 90 | www.hotelzurpost. info | Moderate*

INFORMATION

TOURISMUS SALZBURG GMBH
Auerspergstr. 6 | 5020 Salzburg | tel. 0662 88 98 70; Mozartplatz 5 | tel. 0662 88 98 73 30 | www.salzburg.info

WHERE TO GO

HALLEIN (139 E1) (*⊞ J5*)

The centre of this old salt-mining city on the Salzach River is well worth visiting itself but most people head for the Dürrenberg that was settled by the Celts. It is possible to spend many pleasant hours here in the ● *model mine* and *Celt Village (Ramsaustr. 3 | Bad Dürrnberg | www.salz welten.at)*. *20km (12mi) from Salzburg*

WERFEN (139 E2) (*⊞ J5*)

This market village is famous for its mighty ☀ *Fortress (May–Sept daily 9am–5pm, April, Oct, Nov 9.30am–4pm, April closed Mon | entrance fee 10.50, with lift 14 euros |*

A relaxing boat excursion on Lake Zell

www.salzburg-burgen.at), which has stood proudly on a steep rocky peak high above the Salzach Valley for more than 900 years. A visit to the ● world's largest ice cave *(May–Oct daily 9am–3.30pm | entrance fee 9, with cable car 20 euros | www.eisriesenwelt.at)*, where there are winter-like temperatures at the height of summer, is another highlight of any trip to Werfen. You will see amazing ice formations and palaces of crystalline beauty.

ZELL AM SEE

(139 D3) *(⑰ H6)* This small town (pop. 9600) in the heart of Salzburg Province lies picturesquely on the shore of the more than 1.8mi² large Zellersee that makes it easy to have fun swimming in water that is clean enough to drink.
The Schmittenhöhe (1965 m/6447ft) towers above the shore and the snow-covered peaks of even higher mountains can be seen in the background. The inner city of Zell am See is small but very spruce; a typical market town in the Alps. Its location makes Zell an ideal starting point for excursions into the mountainous regions of the Hohe Tauern, the Salzburg Limestone Mountains and Kitzbühel Alps. This is also

the end of the end of the journey over the *Großglockner Hochalpenstraße (see p. 100)* for those driving from Carinthia.

(see p. 100)

SIGHTSEEING

VOGTTURM LOCAL HERITAGE MUSEUM
The first documentary evidence of the tower goes back to 926; it served to defend the small pre-medieval monastic settlement named Cella in Bisontio that gradually developed into the market of Zell am See. Today, this is the site of the city museum. *May–mid-Oct, Christmas–Easter Mon–Fri 1.30–5pm | Stadtplatz | 3.30 euros*

SCHMITTENHÖHE
Can you reach the top of the mountain (1965m/6447ft) in just 7.1 minutes? The Schmittenhöhe cable car makes it possible! The 360-degree panoramic view sweeps across thirty peaks that are more than 3000m (10,000ft) high – including the Großglockner, Austria's highest mountain. There is a nice easy hike along the Panorama-Höhenpromenade (Panoramic Alpine Promenade) that we can recommend, which is equipped with many signposts and high-powered telescopes. In addition, an enormous artistic space called the 'Gallery on the Slopes' has been created

here where more than twenty large-size sculptures are on permanent display. There are free guided hikes in summer *(www.schmitten.at)*.

FOOD & DRINK

GASTHAUS & KONDITOREI ZUR SALZACHBRÜCKE
This cheerful guesthouse, which is both a pastry shop and down-to-earth inn, is located directly on the Tauernradweg (Tauern cycle path). Specialities from the Pinzgau region (game, trout, cheese). *Closed Mon | Salzachuferstr. 1 | tel. 06542 5 79 76 | Budget–Moderate*

PINZGAUER HÜTTE ≈
You have to work hard before being rewarded with high-calorie, home-made specialities such as *Kaiserschmarrn* (Emperor's pancakes) or *Kasnock'n* (cheese gnocchi): the shortest route is over the Schmittenhöhe top station *(signposted | around 30min downhill)*. Sunny terrace with a view of the Großglockner. *June–Oct, Christmas–Easter | tel. 06549 78 61 | www.pinzgauer-huette.at | Budget–Moderate*

SHOPPING

A large selection of 🙂 goods from local farms is available at the *weekly market* on Stadtplatz *(May–Oct Fri 8am–2pm)*. There is also an impressive selection at the delicatessen *Feinkost Lumpi (Mon–Sat | Seegasse 6)*. If you need to bring your mountaineering gear up-to-date, you are sure to find all you need in the striking new lifestyle sport shop *Intersport Bründl* in Kaprun.

SPORTS & ACTIVITIES

ALPINE SPORTS
The Schmittenhöhe is a first-rate skiing area. For those who need even more: the season in the glacier world of the (3029 m/9938ft) Kitzsteinhorn lasts for ten full months *(www.kitzsteinhorn.at)*.

However, even if you don't have skis on your feet, it is worth making the trip up to the top; on hot days, you will be able to hike in pleasantly fresh conditions. The *Ice Arena* with slides, a snow beach and ice bar *(July, Aug)* is a real highlight. And of course, hikers will find more than

HOHE TAUERN NATIONAL PARK

Untamed alpine landscapes and areas that have been cultivated by mountain farmers for centuries are the two main aspects of Austria's first national park that was established in 1981 and, after a series of enlargements, is now the largest conservation area in the entire alpine region. The single protected area of 716mi² in the provinces of Carinthia, Salzburg and Tyrol is home to around 10,000 animal species and 1800 different varieties of plants from the chamois

and golden eagle to the black vanilla orchid. Something else that makes the Hohe Tauern National Park so special is that it includes a great range of different habitats between the valley and an altitude of well over 3000m (10,000ft). In the wildest sections it appears to have remained untouched. Hollywood has even been there; parts of 'Seven Years in Tibet' were filmed in the national park. Many different excursions guided by the park's rangers *(www.hohetauern.at)*.

enough to keep them happy around Zell am See; that does not mean that cyclists are not taken care of – they can choose between routes for families in the valley, challenging mountain bike trails and even a biker park and downhill stretch on the Maiskogel. The toboggan run on the Maiskogel is open all year round. For those who want to have it especially cushy: ☺ it is possible to hire e-bikes at 23 stations in the Zell am See-Kaprun region.

The already extremely wide range of sporting activities available in the region is rounded off with two eighteen-hole championship golf courses, and paragliding from the Schmitten.

WATER AND ICE

The water in the lake reaches a temperature of 24°C (75°F) at the height of the summer. The three beaches in Zell am See, Thumersbach and Seespitz are excellently equipped – from slides to water-ski schools – and even have heated pools for days that are not so warm. In Kaprun, the modern ● *Tauern Spa* offers health with a view in an area of 12 acres – a fabulous alternative after the bathing season has come to an end *(www.tauernspakaprun. com)*. In winter, skaters flash across the surface of the frozen lake.

WHERE TO STAY

INSIDER TIP ▶ BIO-PENSION HUBERTUS ☺

Sustainability all day long – from the lavish organic, Fairtrade breakfast to the bed linen that is washed with environmentally friendly, biodegradable laundry detergents. The hotel is powered exclusively with eco-electricity and the sustainable warmth comes from a pellets oven and solar power plant. *20 rooms | Gartenstr. 4 | tel. 06542 72427 | www.hubertus-pension.at | Budget*

MAVIDA BALANCE HOTEL & SPA
This wellness hotel, only a few minutes' walk from the valley station of the Schmittenbahn, is one of the loveliest and best of its kind in Austria and has already won international awards. Although it is a design hotel, great importance was placed on reduced aesthetics that radiate tranquillity. *47 rooms | Kirchenweg 11 | tel. 06542 5410 | www.mavida.at | Moderate– Expensive*

INFORMATION

TOURISTENINFORMATION ZELL AM SEE
Brucker Bundestraße 1a | 5700 Zell am See | tel. 06542 720 32 | www.zellamsee-kaprun.com

WHERE TO GO

GIPFELWELT 3000 (PEAK WORLD)
� ● (139 D3) *(Ø H6)*
The Kitzsteinhorn is not only a splendid area for skiing. From the highest panorama platform in the province, visitors are presented with breathtaking views into the valley of Kaprun, of Zellersee and of the – already familiar – thirty three-thousand metre peaks. After that, there is a 360m (1181ft)-tunnel, with information boards on the alpine habitat, through the mountain to another platform; here even ill-prepared tourists in sandals are able to get a view of some really high mountains. There is also a cinema that shows a film giving impressions of the region as the seasons change. *Valley Station Kaprun | Ticket incl. cable car 29.50 euros, from 2pm 22 euros | www.kitzsteinhorn.at | 9 (6mi) from Zell am See*

GLOCKNER-KAPRUN POWER PLANT
(139 D3) *(Ø H6)*
This alpine power plant was opened in 1955 and is a symbol of Austria's recovery

after the Second World War. Although the gigantic concrete walls with a height of 107m (351ft) that curve 494m (1621ft) between the rocks appear intimidating: ⏱ the 5,650 million ft³ of water produce absolutely clean electricity. Ascent with shuttle buses. Tours of the reservoir into the interior of the wall *(daily 10am–3.15pm every 45 min | ca. 1 hr. | departure point Kiosk Mooserboden-Speicher | 5.50 euros)*, modern, interactive *Erlebniswelt Strom & Eis (Electricity & Ice Experiential World)*, hiking trails. *End of May–mid-Oct daily 8.10am–4.45pm (last ascent 3.30pm) | shuttle buses from Kesselfall Alpenhaus | Kaprun | return trip 19 euros.* Safely back at the bottom, you can visit ● the power plant itself and see all of the activity in the turbine house of the Kaprun main stage from a gallery *(daily 8am–6pm | free admission).* www.verbund.com/tm | 16 km (10mi) from Zell am See

KRIMML WATERFALLS ★
(138 C3) (*ɰ G6*)
The falls in the Krimmler Ache Valley, fed by 17 glacier brooks, plummet impressively from a height of 380m (1247ft) over three ledges. This makes them number five on the list of the world's highest waterfalls. A hiking trail takes you directly to this breathtaking spectacle of nature where you will by refreshed by the fine spray of water on your skin and feel the power of the water vibrating in your body. Various lookout posts make it possible for visitors to get spectacular close-up views of the thunderous masses of water *(mid-April–end of Oct | 4 km | approx. 1hr 15min | 2.50 euros).* The *Wasser-Wunder-Welt* at the base of the falls not only uses modern technology to provide visitors with information on the subject of water, they actually come into contact with the refreshing element *(May–Oct daily 9.30am–5pm | 7 euros).* www.wasser

Spectacle of nature in the Hohe Tauern National Park: the Krimml Waterfalls

faelle-krimml.at | 53km (33mi) from Zell am See

NATIONALPARKWELTEN ⏱
(139 D3) (*ɰ H6*)
If you don't intend to go on a hiking tour through the Hohe Tauern National Park *(see Trips & Tours, p. 105)* you should at least make a detour and visit the modern *National Park Centre* in Mittersill. You will be well rewarded for this because you will find out a great deal about life in the region, its geology, flora and fauna, as well as its climate *(Gerlosstr. 18 | Mittersill | daily 9am–6pm | 8.50 euros | www.natio nalparkzentrum.at).* 28 km (17mi) from Zell am See

BURGENLAND/VIENNA/ LOWER AUSTRIA

Vienna has an amazing past record and – as things look today – this is unlikely to change in the years to come. The Austrian capital is one of the most popular destinations worldwide for city trips – with its rich history and magnificent architecture to match, some of which now 'scrapes the sky'.

However, the tempo of the people walking along the streets will show that, in spite of all the developments, Vienna is still not a hectic metropolis. And what was once the centre of a multinational empire satisfies all of its guests' – cultural and culinary – wishes. With the exception of Ödenburg, today's Sopron, the Burgenland, Austria's

youngest province became part of the country after a referendum. The Haydn city of Eisenstadt was chosen to be the province's capital. The landscape of the Burgenland is completely different from the rest of Austria. While the highest elevation, the Geschriebenstein, is a mere 884m (2900ft) high, this is than made up for by the Neusiedlersee/Seewinkel National Park that attracts many visitors with its fascinating flora and fauna.

Lower Austria, the largest of Austria's nine provinces, is the homeland of the Babenberg dynasty and the nucleus of the country. Until St Pölten was elected its capital in 1986, Lower Austria was administered

Vienna and in the meantime Lower Austria and the Burgenland are now in the centre of Europe as a result of the EU expansion

from Vienna that is entirely surrounded by it. The province is divided into four *Viertel* or quarters: the *Wald- und Weinviertel* (Wood and Wine Quarters) north of the Danube managed to preserve much of their original character as a result of their proximity to the former Iron Curtain and need to be explored at leisure while the *Mostviertel* (Cider Quarter) in the south-west is renowned for its excellent fer-

mented pear juice. Lower Austria is alpine in the south and its mountains are also an ideal area for hiking novices.

BADEN

(135 D5) *(ŒŒ Q3)* **In former times, people went to Baden (pop. 25,200) to 'take the waters' or to live after their retirement.**

This is where the flowers bloom: Rosarium in Baden

The charming spa city, which smells of sulphur in some sections, in the foothills of the Anninger has preserved much of the flair of the late 19th century: surrounded by vineyards and characterised architecturally by the Biedermeier period, a visit to the small old section of the town is like a journey back in time.

SIGHTSEEING

ARNULF RAINER MUSEUM
The Arnulf Rainer Museum has been housed in the former Frauenbad (Ladies Bath) since 2009. The internationally renowned contemporary artist was born in Baden in 1929. *Daily except Tue 10am–6pm (Wed to 8pm) | entrance fee 6 euros | Josefsplatz 5 | www.arnulf-rainer.museum.at*

DOBLHOFFPARK
Austria's largest rose garden can be found in the public Doblhoffpark in Baden; the blooms are particularly spectacular in the period between June and October. A good 600 different varieties of roses flower on the more than 30,000 bushes in the 175 beds of the Rosarium. *Helenenstr. 2*

THERMALSTRANDBAD (THERMAL BATH BEACH) ●
Baden actually offers a beach with sand. The second attraction, after the almost Mediterranean bathing fun, is the magnificent Jugendstil architecture of the open air swimming-pool that was inserted so boldly into the Biedermeier town. Gigantic pools for swimming or just having fun as well as hot, sulphur springs, diving tower and slides. *End of April–end of Sept daily from 8.30am | from 6 euros | Helenenstr. 19–21*

FOOD & DRINK

CAFÉ-RESTAURANT DOBLHOFFPARK
Classic Viennese cuisine in pretty surroundings and at very moderate prices. *Mid-May–mid-Nov daily | Pelzgasse 1 | tel. 02252 20 64 21 | Budget–Moderate*

SPORTS & ACTIVITIES

The *Grand Casino Baden* claims to be the most beautiful casino in Europe *(daily 3pm–3 am | Im Kurpark | www.casinos.at)*. When the weather is fine, you should definitely visit the *Strandbad* and otherwise the *Römertherme (www.roemertherme.at)* offers a good option.

WHERE TO STAY

HOTEL HERZOGHOF

The hotel has a prominent position opposite the Kurpark and Casino. However, only the exterior is as old and venerable as it appears; the interior has been carefully revitalised, and the rooms glow in delicate shades of orange. *32 rooms | Kaiser-Franz-Ring 10 | tel. 02252 8 72 97 | www.hotel-herzoghof.at | Moderate*

INFORMATION

TOURIST INFORMATION

Brusattiplatz 3 | tel. 02252 22 60 06 00 | www.baden.at

WHERE TO GO

GUMPOLDSKIRCHEN (135 D5) *(ØØ Q3)*

People visit this small town with its idyllic location and favourable climate to enjoy a visit to one of the many wine taverns: a popular one is *Winzer Hasenöhrl* with its rustic, pleasant atmosphere and beautiful garden *(Wiener Str. 24 | tel. 02252 6 24 57 | Budget). 4km (2.5mi) from Baden*

HEILIGENKREUZ (135 D5) *(ØØ P3)*

The Cistercian monastery in the Vienna Woods can look back over almost 900 years of history; this is reflected in the architecture of the complex. The cloisters are especially impressive. *Daily 9am–6pm, Sun from 10am | entrance fee 7.50 euros | guided tours Mon–Sat 10 & 11am, 2, 3 & 4pm, Sun 11am, 2, 3 & 4pm | www.stift-heiligen kreuz.org. 33 km (20mi) from Baden*

MAYERLING CASTLE (135 D5) *(ØØ P3)*

After the suicide of Crown Prince Rudolf and his mistress Mary Vetsera, the former hunting lodge of the Habsburgs was converted into a Carmelite nunnery. At Empress Sisi's request, the high altar of the neo-Gothic chapel that was erected after the tragedy was placed where the bedroom once stood *(daily 9am–1pm, 1.30–6pm, in winter to 5pm | entrance fee 2.80 euros)*. Connoisseurs with a weakness for exquisite cooking will find what they are looking for in the stylishly elegant ambience of the *Hanner* restaurant *(daily | Mayerling 1 | tel. 02258 23 78 | www.hanner.cc | Expensive)*. *14 km (9mi) from Baden*

SEMMERING (134 C6) *(ØØ P5)*

The Semmering Pass (984m/3228ft) separates the so-called Viennese Alps in Lower

Austria from Styria. In the years between the two World Wars, the hilltop town of the same name was still a fashionable and internationally acclaimed climatic spa. Rulers and aristocrats, rich citizens and artists – from the Habsburg Emperor Karl to the painter Oskar Kokoschka – regularly stayed here. Today, most people just come for a day of skiing or for a long weekend of hiking. What has remained from the golden days of the past is a nostalgic setting of villas and spa hotels, as well as the dramatic mountain landscape which can be admired out of the train window. The trip on the world's first mountain railway (Unesco World Heritage Site) can be easily combined with a pleasant hike along the *Bahnwanderweg* trail. You take the train to the top and then walk down along the embankment – depending on where you start, the walk is 9.5 km/6mi (Breitenstein), 15.5 km/9.5mi (Klamm) or 21 km/13mi (Payerbach). *Trains several times daily | www.semmeringbahn.at*

If you want to enjoy the fresh air in the thickly wooded area for a bit longer, you should check in to the ☺ ❄ INSIDER TIP Bio-Panoramahotel *Wagner*, which is run entirely on ecological principles and offers sensational views *(21 rooms | Hochstr. 267 | tel. 02664 25120 | www.panoramahotel-wagner.at | Moderate). 68 km (42mi) from Baden*

KREMS

(134 B3) (ᗝ O2) The city of Krems is located downstream at the edge of the Wachau, one of the most beautiful Danube landscapes.

On your walk through the 1000-year-old town, you will be able to admire the ensemble of medieval houses in Krems and adjoining Stein. One of the most beautiful buildings is the *Gozzoburg*, in Krems

that was constructed in the 13th century modelled on Italian palazzi. Its INSIDER TIP unique frescoes can be inspected during a special guided tour *(www.weinstadtmuseum.at)*. The district of *Stein* is famous for its so-called 'art mile' with the Kunsthalle, Caricature Museum and Church of the Friars Minor, as well as the Danube University whose students add a touch of youthful flair to the city.

SIGHTSEEING

CARICATURE MUSEUM

This building, which was designed by Gustav Peichl, is (as the name says) devoted to caricatures and offers visitors profound insights into the Austrian soul. There are frequent temporary exhibitions in addition to the permanent show of works by Manfred Deix and Ironimus (Gustav Peichl's nom de plume). *Daily 10am–6pm | entrance fee 10 euros | Steiner Landstr. 3 a | www.karikaturmuseum.at*

KUNSTHALLE

The former tobacco factory was transformed into a modern exhibition centre where the artworks are not simply presented one next to the other but are sophisticatedly staged. The scope of the works on display ranges from the second half of the 19th century to contemporary art. *Daily 10am–6pm | entrance fee 10 euros (combi-ticket Kulturmeile Krems with the Caricature Museum 13 euros) | Franz-Zeller-Platz 3 | www.kunsthalle.at*

SANDGRUBE 13

The eight stations of this world of wine tour provide an all-round experience including the vineyard, cellar and of course some wine tasting. Can only be visited completely on a guided tour. *Mon–Sat (May–Oct daily) 10am and 2pm | 11 euros | Sandgrube 13 | www.sandgrube13.at*

FOOD & DRINK

JELL

This restaurant is full of character and has a charming proprietor who cooks her hearty food with a great deal of creativity. *Sat/Sun only for lunch, Mon closed | Hoher Markt 8–9 | tel. 02732 8 23 45 | Moderate–Expensive*

ZUM ELEFANTEN ☺

Chic restaurant in vaulted rooms. The host and chef have a great deal of international experience that they pass on at pleasing prices. Healthy food made with organic products. *Mon, Tue, Sun afternoon closed | Schürerplatz 9 | Krems-Stein | tel. 02732 8 50 16 | www.zum-elefanten.at | Moderate*

SHOPPING

Excellent wines (Grüner Veltliner and Riesling) are grown in the Wachau and nearby Krems Valley region. In addition, this is the home of the protected Wachau apricots and a festival is held in their honour in Krems in mid-July. *(www.alles-marille.at).*

SPORTS & ACTIVITIES

The region around Krems is perfect for cycle tours. In addition to the cycle path along the Danube, there are pleasant routes into the Krems Valley, Kamp Valley and Waldviertel. For those who want a more leisurely way to explore the area, there are several ● ship excursions through the Wachau every day *(www.ddsg-blue-danube.at).*

WHERE TO STAY

WEINGUT NIGL

The estate run by the famous Nigl family of winegrowers is located a short distance

Medieval flair:
Stein Gate in Krems

outside of Krems in idyllic Senftenberg (9km/5.5mi). It has been perfectly revitalised with a fairy-tale inner garden, sensationally beautiful rooms, exquisite cuisine and is surrounded by vineyards. *11 rooms | Kirchenberg 1 | Senftenberg | tel. 02719 2 60 95 00 | www.weingutnigl.at | Moderate*

WEINGUT ZÖHRER ☺

Live with a wine-growing family with a long tradition in the middle of the vines. Rooms with natural wood furniture, sunbathing lawn and pool in the garden. *10 rooms | Sandgrube 1 | tel. 02732 8 31 91 | www.zoehrer.at | Budget*

INFORMATION

KREMS TOURISMUS

Utzstr. 6 | 3500 Krems | tel. 02732 8 26 76 | www.krems.info

WHERE TO GO

ARCHE NOAH (NOAH'S ARK) ☺
(134 B3) (*∅ O2*)

For more than 20 years, this organisation has devoted itself to preserving the great variety of cultivated plants – so far, more than 6000 old varieties have been saved from extinction. The Arche Noah has its home in the *Baroque Schiltern Castle* with its lovingly cared for display garden. There are frequent tours and special ones with tastings twice a year *(April–Oct Tue–Fri 10am–4pm, Sat, Sun to 6pm | 6 euros | www.arche-noah.at)*. You can also shop here and there is no entrance fee for that. There are another 18 gardens along the Kamp River that can be visited and will delight all garden lovers *(www.diegaerten.at)*. 16km (10mi) from Krems

GÖTTWEIG (134 B3–4) (*∅ O2*)

The Benedictine monastery, which dominates the landscape from the top of a densely wooded hill, can be seen from miles away. The monastery was founded in 1074 and rebuilt in the Baroque style after 1718 following plans drawn up by the architect Lukas von Hildebrandt after it had been destroyed by a fire. The main highlights are the imperial staircase with a fresco by Paul Troger on the ceiling, the two-towered collegiate church with altar paintings by Kremser Schmidt and other artists, and the graphics cabinet; with its 28,000 works, this is the largest private collection of its kind in Austria. *Daily | 10am–6pm | from 7 euros | www.stift goettweig.or.at. 5km (3mi) from Krems*

LANGENLOIS (134 B3) (*∅ O2*)

This small town is the capital of the Kamp Valley wine-growing region *(www.kamp tal.at)*. An ultra-modern cube can be seen from afar rising up from among the vines: it is the visitors' centre of the ● *Loisium*, a sort of experiential world of wine that does full justice to its name. Here, in the more than 900-year-old subterranean vaults, interested visitors are shown how still and sparkling wine are made and are given a wealth of information on the cultural history of wine and the way wine-growers lived in times gone by *(daily 10am–7pm | 11.50 euros | www.loisium-weinwelt.at)*. A state-of-the-art spa hotel is part of the complex *(82 rooms | Loisium Allee 2 | tel. 02734 7 71 00 | www.loisiumlanenois.at | Expensive)*. 11km (7mi) from Krems

MELK ★ (134 B4) (*∅ O3*)

The building, which was designed by Jakob Prandtauer and completed in 1736, high above the Danube replaced a monastery from the 12th century. Melk developed into a centre of European intellectual life in the Middle Ages. The path from the abbey church, via the library and into the former imperial rooms where the museum is located today leads from one revelation to the next *(daily 9am–4.30pm | entrance fee 9.50 euros | www.stiftmelk.at)*. 36km (22mi) from Krems

MOSTVIERTEL (CIDER QUARTER)
(133 E–F5) (*∅ M3–4*)

The south-western corner of Lower Austria becomes submerged in a sea of white blossoms when the thousands of apple and pear trees come into flower in April. But, it is also beautiful in this peaceful rural landscape in summer when the cider inns open their terraces for their thirsty guests: a good address is ☺ INSIDER TIP *Hansbauer (depending on the time of year, open Thu, Fri from 4pm, Sat, Sun from 3pm | Krottendorf | www.hansbauer.at)*, who produces his cider from fruit from his own orchards of mixed fruit trees. The old trading centre Waidhofen an der Ybbs is especially worth visiting as are the *Erlebnismuseum Ferrum* in Ybbsitz, which is de-

Nobody regrets making a stop in Weissenkirchen in the Wachau

voted to the tradition of the blacksmith *(daily | 6.60 euros | www.ferrum-ybbsitz.at)* and the *Ostarrichi Kulturhof* in Neuhofen an der Ybbs *(April–Oct Thu–Tue | 3 euros | www.ostarrichi-kulturhof.at)*: Neuhofen was in the centre of the property of a deed of gift from 996 in which the name Ostarrichi is mentioned for the first time – consequently, this museum is entirely devoted to the history of the country in the Middle Ages. *www.mostvietel.info. 82km/51mi (from Neuhofen)*

ST PÖLTEN (134 B4) *(𝄜 O3)*

Austria's youngest province capital (pop. 52,000) is a fascinating melange of the Baroque old city where the architect Jakob Prandtauer left his mark and a hypermodern government district with a Festival Hall, the Province Museum and Klangturm (Sound Tower). You should start your tour by taking the free tourist train through the inner city *(Thu–Sat 10am–5pm at hourly intervals from the Tourist Information Office on Rathausplatz)*, and then strolling leisurely through the modern province parliament district *(www.st-poelten.gv.at)*. *32km (20mi) from Krems*

WACHAU ⭐ (134 B3–4) *(𝄜 O2–3)*

The Danube carved a narrow 30km (19mi) valley between Melk and Krems and, in the process, created one of the most beautiful river landscapes in Europe. In 2000, the Wachau became a Unesco World Heritage site. The Wachau is well known for its vineyards, idyllic wine-growing villages that have preserved their medieval character, apricot orchards, and massive castle and monastery complexes. The most important sights include the ⚜ *Aggstein castle ruins,* which overlook the northern bank from on top of a narrow 300m (985ft)-high cliff *(March–Oct. daily. 9am–6pm, June–Aug to 7pm, Nov. Sat/Sun 9am–5pm | entrance fee 6.50 euros | www.ruineaggstein.at). Weißenkirchen*, with its fortified church and the Teisenhoferhof, one of the most beautiful Renaissance courtyards in the region, is well worth making a stop to visit *(www.weissenkirchen.at). Spitz* is another picturesque market village and attracts many visitors to its colourful *Apricot Festival* on the second to last weekend in July. The high point of any tour of the Wachau is *Dürnstein.* The most beautiful view is from the river; to experience this, take the INSIDER TIP ferry to Rossatz on the opposite bank and you will have plenty of time to really enjoy the scenery. You can avoid all of the tourists in tiny Dürnstein if you climb up to the ☀ castle ruins where King Richard the Lionheart was held prisoner in the 12th century. The Gothic charnel house, medieval pillory and monastery church are three of the village's highlights. A tip if you want to spend the night: the *Schlosshotel Dürnstein (47 rooms | tel. 02711 2 12 | www.schloss.at | Expensive)* is an exquisite place to lay your head. A tip for a tipple: the *Alte Klosterkeller (Mon–Fri from 3pm, Sat/Sun from noon | Anzuggasse 237 | www.alter-klosterkeller.at | Budget)* is a *heuriger* in a dreamlike setting. On hot days, you can take a ● dip in the Danube free of charge – and enjoy the breathtaking backdrop, e.g. on the border between Unter- und Oberloiben, where there is also a large car park where the Danube Road curves inland for a short distance. Once you park your car, it is only a two-minute walk to the beach. For something more exerting, try a hike on the *Welterbesteig (World Heritage Trail) (www.welterbesteig.at)* or *Donauradweg (Danube Cycle Track)*. The midsummer festival is another highlight on the Wachau's calendar of events *(www.sonnenwende.at). www.wachau.at. 3km (2mi) from Krems*

NEUSIEDLER SEE (LAKE NEUSIEDL)

(135 E–F 5–6) (𝑚 R4) The gigantic steppe lake, which the Burgenland and Hungary share, is the ocean of the Viennese. This is where Austria opens up into the Pannonian lowlands that have a strong **effect on Burgenland's culture and also bring it many climatic advantages.**

In summer, the warm water in the lake makes it an inviting place for a swim and the – usually fairly respectable – breeze makes it ideal for sailing and surfing as early as April. In winter, the lake freezes and becomes an enormous natural ice-skating rink. Podersdorf on the eastern shore is the hot spot for a summer holiday, Neusiedl am See on the northern edge is a very popular meeting place for yachtsmen, while villages such as Rust and Mörbisch on the western shore are more suited for contemplative relaxation between the vineyards, typical Pannonian lanes and the lake. The Neusiedler See/Seewinkel National Park in the south near Illmitz has been created to protect the special flora and fauna of the region. Mörbisch and Illmitz are only 60km (37mi) away from each other. Unesco declared the entire area a World Heritage Site in 2001.

SIGHTSEEING

MÖRBISCH

The typical arcaded houses and long narrow lanes exude a special Pannonian flair. Mörbisch is especially famous in Austria for its large stage in the lake on which spectacular operetta performances take place in summer. *www.moerbischamsee.at*

NEUSIEDLER SEE/SEEWINKEL NATIONAL PARK ★ ☺

This is an area where various different landscapes come together; where the Alps make one last curve before running into the Small Pannonian Plain. Alpine, Pannonian, Asian, Mediterranean and Nordic influences can all be felt here and that explains the great biodiversity. The area has been protected as a cross-border national park since 1993. Cycle paths, hiking trails and guided tours make it possible for visitors to become better acquainted with the region (bird watching!) and, in recent years, old domestic-animal races, such as Hungarian grey cattle, Mangalitza pigs and white donkeys, have once again started grazing peacefully among the reeds. The visitors' centre in Illmitz is a good place to get first-hand information *(April–Oct Mon–Fri 8am–5pm, Sat, Sun 10am–5pm, Nov–March Mon–Fri 8am–4pm | Hauswiese | www.nationalpark-neusiedlersee-seewinkel.at)*.

RUST

The smallest town in Austria (pop. 1900) is flanked by vineyards on one side and by a belt of reeds with a good 1km (1000 yard)-wide path through them to a lakeside beach on the other. Rust is the home of a wine academy and many visitors also show great interest in the stork nests on the chimneys that are occupied by the same 'guests' year after year. The charming family homes with their Renaissance and Baroque façades are very-well preserved. *www.rust.at*

INSIDER TIP **TOMATEN STEKOVICS** ☺

Erich Stekovics collected tomato seeds from all over the world in his search for long-lost taste. Today, more than 3200 varieties grow on his fields near the lake – it is the largest tomato collection in the world and the plants flourish in the mild climate of the region. Erich Stekovics, the 'Emperor of the *Paradeiser*' (tomatoes are called *Paradeiser*, or 'apples of paradise' in Austria) personally leads visitors through the great diversity of his collection. *July–Sept daily 4pm (by advance booking only) | 45 euros (incl. 15-euro voucher for goods) | Schäferhof 13 | Frauenkirchen | tel. 0676 9 66 07 05 | www.stekovics.at*

FOOD & DRINK

GASTHAUS ZUR DANKBARKEIT

The culinary larder overflows with the products of the Seewinkel: an unsurpassed selection of tomatoes and capsicums, Mangalitza pigs, grey cattle and free-range goose, pike-perch and other fish from the lake are prepared superbly

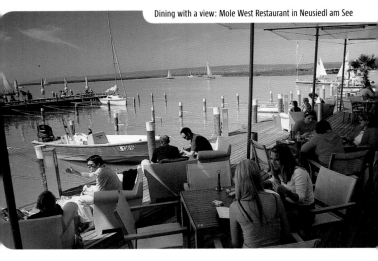

Dining with a view: Mole West Restaurant in Neusiedl am See

Stately building with the flair of a spa hotel: Esterházy Palace in Eisenstadt

here and served in an ambience that is just as lovely. *Wed, Thu closed | Hauptstr. 39 | Podersdorf | tel. 02177 22 23 | www. dankbarkeit.at | Moderate*

MOLE WEST

This is the place to experience Pannonian joie-de-vivre in a stylish package. Interesting cuisine, good wines, and fabulous sunsets. *Daily, April–Nov 9am–midnight, different, shorter opening hours in winter | See-gelände 9, Neusiedl am See | tel. 02167 2 02 05 | www.molewest.at | Moderate*

STECKERLFISCH JANDL

Steckerlfisch – whole fish skewered on sticks and grilled over charcoal – are an old Pannonian speciality. Today, mackerel are the most common but Jandl also serves freshwater fish such as catfish, char and carp, if desired, smoked over beech wood. *March–Oct daily. | Untere Hauptstr. 86 | Weiden | Tel. 02167 67 77 48 | www. steckerlfisch.at | Budget*

SHOPPING

Wine lovers will be able to purchase a wide variety of red and white vintages at reasonable prices directly from the wine-growers or in the many vinotheques in the Burgenland. The ☺ INSIDER TIP *Weinwerk Burgenland (April–Dec daily 10.30am–7pm | Obere Hauptstr. 31 | Neusiedl am See | www.weinwerk-burgenland.at)* has a very good selection and also sells specialities produced by local farmers such as Mangalitza black pudding and smoked game ham, as well as handicrafts including blue-dyed textiles.

SPORTS & ACTIVITIES

Swimming, sailing, surfing and kayaking in summer; skating, ice-sailing and ice-surfing in winter – there is more than enough to do! However, the broad reed belt means that it is only possible to actually reach the water at places where beaches have been established. These can be found in Illmitz, Podersdorf, Weiden, Neusiedl am See, Breitenbrunn, Rust and Mörbisch. The region is too flat for serious hiking but this makes it perfect for cycle tours, although there is often a strong wind which can make it rather strenuous. The terrain is ideal for horse riding and equestrian fans have around 1300km (800mi) of trails at their disposal.

WHERE TO STAY

GERTRUDE LINDER
Spacious, bright rooms and holiday flats, well-cared-for garden with many old trees. *5 rooms | Kalvarienbergstr. 30 | Neusiedl am See | tel. 0699 111264 63 | www. tiscover.com/gertrude.linder | Budget*

ST MARTINS THERME UND LODGE
The name 'lodge' was chosen quite consciously; St Martins considers itself not merely a fabulous hotel with a spa but also the starting point for tours to discover all the area has to offer. Excellent birdwatching programme with expert rangers. *150 rooms| Im Seewinkel 1 | Frauenkirchen | tel. 02172 2 05 00 | www. stmartins.at | Expensive*

INSIDER TIP ▸ WINZERHOF ELFRIEDE KAZDA
Stay in a traditional vineyard environment and spend the night sleeping in rooms with old wooden furniture. A holiday cannot be much better than this – and that, at prices just like they were 15 years ago! *Markt 11 | Weiden | tel. 0664 5 50 99 37 | www.urlaub-am-winzerhof.at | Budget*

INFORMATION

NEUSIEDLER SEE TOURISMUS
Obere Hauptstr. 24 | Neusiedl am See | tel. 02167 86 00 | www.neusiedlersee.com

WHERE TO GO

EISENSTADT (135 E6) *(𝄐 Q4)*
The province capital located at the foot of the Leitha Mountains is inseparably linked with the names Esterházy and Haydn. The palace in Eisenstadt is the ancestral seat of the Hungarian Esterházy dynasty of princes who were presented with the whole city by Emperor Ferdinand II in 1622. From outside, the palace with its beautiful park has the appearance of a time-honoured spa hotel. The interior however is all the more luxurious. The hall named after the Austrian composer Joseph Haydn (1732–1809) in which he performed his duties as court musician for so many years is especially worth seeing *(April–beginning of Nov daily 10am–6pm | 9 euros | www. schloss-esterhazy.at)*. The symbol of the charming city is the Bergkirche (Mountain Church) with the Haydn Mausoleum. *www. eisenstadt-tourismus.at*

VIENNA

MAP INSIDE BACK COVER
(135 D–E4) *(𝄐 Q3)* 'We might not have an emperor these days, but at least

CITY ▸ WHERE TO START?
Start your visit of Vienna on **Stephansplatz (U D3)** *(𝄐 d3)*, the heart of the city. Climb one of the towers – or take the lift – to get a good bird's eye view of all the narrow streets of the inner city. Follow this with a visit to the cathedral before you set out on a lengthy stroll to discover all of the sights of the city. Stephansplatz can be reached by underground (lines 1, 3) and there is also an underground car park.

we've got his crown jewels'. This slogan reflects how Vienna views its role in history. Today the city has a lively music, musical and theatrical scene that, along with the great variety of gastronomic establishments with countless restaurants, cafés and pubs – here, they are called *Beiseln* – make up the unique atmosphere of the city.

Many palaces in the inner city have been renovated in recent years and the grey feeling that clung to Vienna has disappeared completely. There is an excellent network of public transport *(www.wiener linien.at)* that makes it easy to do without a car and, in any case, it is easier to explore the inner city on foot. You will find more detailed information in the MARCO POLO guide: 'Vienna'.

SIGHTSEEING

ALBERTINA
(U C4–5) (ᴑ c4–5)

Since its expansion, the Albertina has become one of the big crowd-pullers among Vienna's museums. The collection, which was started by Duke Albert von Sachsen-Teschen, comprises 50,000 drawings and one million prints from the late Gothic period to modern times. Among them are Dürer's 'Praying Hands' and 'Field Rabbit' but they are not permanently on display. The former Habsburg apartments, with a more than 120m (394ft) long suite of rooms and a view of the Burggarten (Castle Garden), is a rare example of Classicist state rooms in Vienna. *Daily 10am–6pm, Wed to 9pm | entrance fee*

Equestrian monument in front of the Albertina on Albertinaplatz

11 euros | Albertinaplatz 3 | www.albertina. at | U 1, 2, 4: Karlsplatz, trams 1, 2, D: Oper

BELVEDERE (0) (🗺 Q3)

The *Upper Belvedere,* where Prince Eugene of Savoy the man who saved Vienna from the Turks once lived and where Austria's sovereignty was sealed in 1955, houses an extensive collection of works by Gustav Klimt as well as Austrian masterpieces from the 19th and 20th centuries by Waldmüller, Schwind, Schiele, Kokoschka and many other artists. Medieval art is displayed in the *Prunkstall (Palace Stables)* and the living and reception rooms of Prince Eugene can be visited in the *Lower Belvedere.* *Upper Belvedere: daily 10am–6pm, Lower Belvedere: daily 10am–6pm, Wed to 9pm, Palace Stables daily 10am–noon | Prinz-Eugen-Str. 27 | Rennweg 6 | combi-ticket 16 euros | www.belvedere.at | tram D: Schloss Belvedere, 71: Lower Belvedere*

HOFBURG (IMPERIAL PALACE) ⭐
(U B–C 4–5) (🗺 b–c 4–5)

No other building gives a greater impression of the extent of the Habsburg's power than the Hofburg. Today, the Hofburg, which expanded over centuries to become the present complex, is the official residence of the Federal President, a congress centre and also the home of a countless number of sumptuously decorated halls of state and museums. The National Library, with its fascinatingly spectacular State Hall is part of it, as is the Spanish Riding School, the Imperial Chapel where the Vienna Boy's Choir performs at high mass on Sunday, the Silver Collection and the Treasury, where not only the crown of the Emperor of the Holy Roman Empire, but also the treasure of the Order of the Golden Fleece, is on display. No Habsburg ruler used the same rooms as his predecessor. The apartments occupied by the eccentric Empress Sisi in the Ame-

lientrakt are very popular – especially her gymnasium and dressing room. *Tramlines 1, 2, D: Burgring, bus 2 A: Heldenplatz*

KARLSKIRCHE (ST CHARLES' CHURCH) (U D6) (🗺 d6)

Construction of the most important Baroque church in Vienna, with its 72m (236ft)-high dome, was begun by Johann Bernhard Fischer von Erlach and completed by his son Joseph Emanuel. The large pond with the statue by Henry Moore in front of it makes a fascinating contrast to the church's façade. *U 1, 2, 4: Karlsplatz*

KUNSTHAUS (0) (🗺 Q3)

'All of Hundertwasser' is the motto of the multipurpose house where the world's only permanent exhibition of works by the fantastic realist Friedensreich Hundertwasser is on display. *Daily 10am–7pm | entrance fee 9 euros | Untere Weißgerberstr. 13 | www.kunsthauswien.at | tramline 1: Radetzkyplatz*

KUNSTHISTORISCHES MUSEUM (U B5) (🗺 b5)

Gottfried Semper's building, which was opened in 1891, houses the antique and oriental-Egyptian collection along with the famous gallery of paintings. The foundation to the collection was formed in the middle of the 17th century with Archduke Leopold Wilhelm's collection of Venetian and Flemish masters. *Tue–Sun 10am–6pm, Thu to 9pm | entrance fee 12 euros | Maria-Theresien-Platz | www.khm.at | U 2: Museumsquartier*

MUSEUMSQUARTIER ⭐ ●
(U A–B5) (🗺 a–b5)

The Museumsquartier, or MQ for short, is one of the ten largest cultural complexes in the world. It houses many autonomous cultural initiatives but they are overshadowed by two museums of international importance: The *Museum Leopold (Wed–Mon 10am–6pm, Thu to 9pm | 11 euros | www.leopoldmuseum.org)* presents a panorama of Austrian art since the late 19th century including the world's largest collection of paintings by Egon Schiele and many masterpieces by Gustav Klimt. Different sections of the comprehensive collection of international twentieth-century art are shown in the temporary exhibitions held at the *Museum Moderner Kunst Stiftung Ludwig – MuMok (Mon 2–7pm, Tue–Sun 10am–7pm, Thu to 9pm | 9 euros | www.mumok.at)*. The cafés and sofas in the inner courtyard of the MQ have achieved cult status and there are also regular free events. *www.mqw.at | U 2: Museumsquartier, Volkstheater*

LOW BUDGET

▶ No entrance fee is charged for the ● *Danube Island Festival* in Vienna. The largest open-air spectacle in Europe takes place every year on a weekend in June on the Danube Island. There is live music for all tastes on the many stages; you will also find more than enough to satisfy your hunger. The highlight is the final fireworks display on Sunday.

▶ The cellar lanes in the *Weinviertel* in Lower Austria are absolutely unique: wine presses are hidden behind the façades of the small houses and, even farther back, cellars have been dug deep into the earth. In summer, the winegrowers organise festivals and give tours of their establishments: wine tasting and a snack are included in the price of 7.50 euros. Information on the dates can be found under: *Weinviertel Tourismus (tel. 02552 3515 | www.weinviertel.at)* and then clicking 'Wein & Kulinarik'. Summer guests who stay in one of the 750 participating enterprises are given the Neusiedler See Card free of charge at one of the local offices; it makes it possible to visit almost 50 of the top recreational facilities from a lakeside beach to a summer matinee at Esterhazy Palace.

NASCHMARKT ● (U B–C6) (*ʃ b–c6*)
The Naschmarkt in Vienna has a long tradition as a market but these days many of the old fruit and vegetable stands have been replaced with restaurants and delis. The Naschmarkt has become the main restaurant strip in Vienna, and you can still have breakfast here at 4pm. A colourful flea market is held on Saturdays. *Mon–Sat 8am–midnight (depending on the weather), flea market Sat 6.30am–6pm | U 4: Kettenbrückengasse, Karlsplatz*

NATURHISTORISCHES MUSEUM (U B4) (*ʃ b4*)
The sheer quantity of exhibits in the geological-paleontological, botanical, zoological and anthropological collections is simple overwhelming. Along with the ancient statue of the 'Venus of Willendorf', the restored dinosaur skeletons are some of the other highlights. *Wed–Mon 9am–6.30pm, Wed to 9pm | entrance fee 10 euros | Maria-Theresien-Platz | www.nhm-wien.ac.at | U 2: Museumsquartier, U 3: Volkstheater*

PRATER (0) (*ʃ Q3*)
Enormous amusement park with the famous ⚜ giant Ferris wheel (61m/200ft in diameter), hypermodern roller coasters and flight simulators. Surrounded by an enormous green recreation area for the Viennese. *U 1: Praterstern*

St Stephan's Cathedral towers up out of the sea of houses

SCHÖNBRUNN ⭐ (0) (🗺 Q3)

The long, yellow Baroque castle is one of the most beautiful in Europe. Forty of the most magnificent of the 1441 rooms in the imperial summer residence can be visited. Other attractions include the 🔭 *Gloriette* as an observation point, the palm house and the world's oldest zoo. You should plan to spend an entire day in the complex. *Castle daily April–June and Sept/Oct 8.30am–5.30pm, Nov–March 8.30am–5pm, July/Aug to 6.30pm (10.50 euros), Zoo daily from 9am, in winter to 4.30pm, in summer to 6.30pm (14 euros) | tickets can be booked online: www.schoenbrunn.at | www.zoovienna.at | U 4: Schönbrunn (Schloss) or Hietzing (Zoo)*

SIGMUND FREUD MUSEUM (0) (🗺 Q3)

The founder of psychoanalysis opened his office on Berggasse in 1891; this is where he carried out his analyses and wrote 'The Interpretation of Dreams' and other works. The museum shows a selection of autographs, documents, photos and objects that were in Freud's personal possession. The waiting room contains the original furnishings. *Berggasse 19 | daily 9am–5pm, July–Sept to 6pm | 8 euros | www.freud-museum.at | U 2: Schottentor*

STEPHANSDOM (ST STEPHAN'S CATHEDRAL) (U D3) (🗺 d3)

St Stephan's Cathedral received the basic form it has today when a second Romanesque church, which was later adapted to the Gothic style, was erected in the early 13th century. The main portal, the two so-called 'Heathen Towers' and west gallery all date from this period. After its completion in 1433, the 136.70m (448.5ft)-high south tower remained the highest church tower in Europe for many years; it is still Austria's highest. A lift takes visitors up to the 🔭 observation platform with a splendid panoramic view over the city. The gigantic 'Pummerin' bell is considered Vienna's symbol in sound; it is only rung to celebrate the highest holidays and on other special occasions. *U 1 and 3: Stephansplatz*

FOOD & DRINK

CAFÉ PRÜCKEL (U F4) *(𝄢 f4)*

The original design from the 1950s surprises first-time visitors to the *Prückel* that is located in a glamorous palatial building on the Ringstrasse. Renowned for its fresh *strudels*; charming garden. *Daily 8.30am–10pm | Stubenring 24 (Luegerplatz) | www.prueckel.at | Budget*

FIGLMÜLLER (U E3) *(𝄢 e3)*

The top address in the first district for *Wiener Schnitzel* (phenomenal!) and everything else Viennese cuisine has to offer. *Daily | Bäckerstr. 6 | tel. 01 5 12 17 60 | www.figlmueller.at | Moderate*

INSIDER TIP ► **NENI** (U C6) *(𝄢 c6)*

Where the in crowd meets on the Naschmarkt. Starting with Hebrew food, Neni serves ethno-cooking from around the world: from Caribbean red lentil soup to New York cheesecake, everything is cooked using recipes the owner collected during his travels. *Daily | Am Naschmarkt 510 | tel. 01 5 85 20 20 | www.neni.at | Budget–Moderate*

STEIRERECK (U E5) *(𝄢 e5)*

For years, the food served in the *Steirereck* has maintained its level of perfection. The location in the Stadtpark (City Park) is the ideal setting for chef Heinz Reitbauer's contemporary Austrian cuisine that is considered to be unquestionably the best in the entire country. *Mon–Fri 11.30am–2.30pm and from 6.30pm | Am Heumarkt 2a (in the Stadtpark) | Burggarten | tel. 01 7 13 31 68 | www.steirereck.at | Expensive*

SHOPPING

The best, but also most expensive, addresses can be found on Kohlmarkt and the Graben, as well as Kärntner Straße. Things are somewhat less expensive on the inner Mariahilfer Straße between the U 2 Museumsquartier underground station and the West Train Station. Many fashion chains have flagship stores here along with the *Gerngroß* and *La Stafa* department stores. Avant-garde fashion designers have moved into the area between Mariahilfer Straße and the Spittelberg where arts and crafts are also sold. Stylists will help you find what you are

CABARET

There is a saying that 'humour is when you laugh in spite of it all'; this is turned into a form of art in the cabaret, and Austria has produced many of its masters. No matter whether they are making fun of politics, personal relationships or sport – the cabaret artists lay bare all of the depths of the human soul with their finely-tuned wit. Vienna is a stronghold of this art and cabaret has a long tradition here. The oldest – and also most famous – venue is the

Simpl (www.simpl.at) where several performers appear on stage every evening. If your German is good enough, you can go to solo programmes by well-known (and some still-to-be-discovered) artists at several intimate establishments such as *Das Niedermair (www.niedermair.at),* the *Orpheum (www.orpheum.at),* the *Kulisse (www.kulisse.at)* or Vienna's newest and largest cabaret theatre, *the Stadtsaal (www.stadtsaal.com).*

The fascinating night-time view of the Sunken City and Uno City

looking for on **INSIDER TIP** guided shopping tours *(www.7tm.at)*. Many of the best antique shops are in the narrow streets of the first district.

ENTERTAINMENT

The *Loos American Bar (Kärntner Durchgang 10)*, *Kruger's American Bar (Krugerstr. 5)*, the *Onyx Bar (Stephansplatz 12, in the Haas Haus)* and *Drings (Kärntner Ring 8, im Hotel The Ring)* are just four of the chicest bars in the Austrian capital.

The student crowd gets together in the Museumsquartier and the Spittelberg; trendsetters head for the Donaukanal for a drink at the **INSIDER TIP** *Strandbar Herrmann* and dinner at the *Motto* or a little bit to the north at the *Summer Stage*. Night owls get drawn to the *Sunken City* on the Danube Island. A vibrant pub scene (with live music) has developed in the arches under the U6 underground line.

The outlying suburbs of Grinzing and Nussdorf are popular with *heuriger* fans. Theatre performances are held in the Burg- and Volks-Theatre, the Theater in der Josefstadt and dozens of smaller venues,

and the State Opera, Volksoper, Musikverein, Konzerthaus and Theater an der Wien are the places to go for excellent music.

WHERE TO STAY

ALMA BOUTIQUEHOTEL
(U E3) (*∅ e3*)

Earth tones – gold, brown and orange – dominate in the chic decoration of this small hotel in an old Jugendstil house. The rooms are not particularly spacious but the hotel is in the heart of town. *26 rooms | Hafnersteig 7 | tel. 01 53 32 96 1-0 | www.hotel-alma.com | Moderate*

BOUTIQUEHOTEL STADTHALLE ☺
(0) (*∅ Q3*)

The new extension to the existing building from the turn of the century makes this the first city hotel worldwide with a zero energy-balance. This means that you will not only have an idyllic stay here but also a clean conscience. Lavender even blooms on the hotel roof. *80 rooms | Hackengasse 20 | tel. 01 9 82 42 72 | www. hotelstadthalle.at | Moderate*

The wine-growing estates of Klosterneuburg are among the oldest in the country

INSIDER TIP ▶ WOMBAT THE NASCHMARKT (U C6) (*Ⳬ c6*)
Budget hostel with a design touch. Top trendy, spotlessly clean, central location, absolutely reasonable prices. Free WiFi in the lobby and breakfast area. *121 rooms | Rechte Wienzeile 35 | tel. 01 8 97 23 36 | www.wombats.eu/vienna | Budget*

INFORMATION

WIEN TOURISMUS
Obere Augartenstr. 40 | 1020 Wien; Tourist Information Office on Albertinaplatz (behind the State Opera) and at the airport | tel. 01 2 45 55 | www.wien.info

WHERE TO GO

CARNUNTUM (135 F4) (*Ⳬ R3*)
The Roman legion's camp near Petronell was founded in the year 6AD. The remains of two *amphitheatres*, the *large public baths,* the *Heidentor (Heathens' Gate)*, the *Museum Carnuntium* and, the centre of the park, the *Petronell Open Air Museum* that covers the civilian city can be visited. Several buildings, including the *Villa Urbana* town house, are faithful reconstructions of the original. Reenacted gladiator fights and other events take place occasionally throughout the season *Open-air sections end of March–Oct, Museum Jan–Oct daily 10am–5pm | entrance fee 10 euros | www.carnuntum.co.at | 40 km (25mi) from Vienna*

KLOSTERNEUBURG (135 D4) (*Ⳬ Q3*)
The *Verdun* Altar, a masterpiece of Romanesque goldsmith art, is one of the highlights in the Medieval section of the 900-year-old monastery. The cloister garden and the labyrinthine wine cellar – the monastery has one of the oldest and largest wine-growing estates in Austria – are also well worth a visit. The monastery occupies an elevated position; down in the Danube wetlands, the *Essl Museum (www.essl.museum)* shows changing exhibitions of contemporary art from Agnes

and Karlheinz Essl's private collection. *www.stift-klosterneuburg.at | 14 km (9mi) from Vienna*

SCHLOSSHOF (135 F4) (*∅ R3*)

Today, the former imperial festival palace, which was bought by Prince Eugene of Savoy in 1726 and expanded by Lukas von Hildebrandt, once again glows in all its Baroque splendour. The terraced park has also been almost completely restored as has the Meierhof farm with its stables for rare domestic animals. The castles of Niederweiden, Orth and Eckartsau are located within a radius of 15km (10mi) in the Marchfeld. *www.schlosshof.at | 65km (40mi) from Vienna*

ZWETTL

(134 A2) (*∅ N2*) **Zwettl (pop. 11,300), the brewery town, is the most important city in the Waldviertel, a unique Austrian landscape with gently rolling hills, dark coniferous forests and deep moors.**

Time seems to have stood still in the small villages scattered throughout the countryside here and the area reminds some people of Scandinavia. In tune with its surroundings, Zwettl has a certain provincial charm.

SIGHTSEEING

MAIN SQUARE

The former triangular market place that the road to Bohemia opens into is the heart of this Kuenring city. It is lined with houses from the 16th and 17th centuries with striking façades; the profiled Renaissance chimney on the left side of the roof of the chemist's house (number 11), with small columns at the corners and which is crowned with volutes, is particularly beautiful. The colourful Hundertwasser Fountain,

which the artist designed for his chosen home for a period, is another eye catcher.

CISTERCIAN MONASTERY ZWETTL

The Zwettl monastery, which was founded by Hadmar von Kuenring in 1138, rises up above a bend in the River Kamp. You can visit the oldest chapter house in Austria, a room from the 12th century whose vaults are supported by a single stone column, the Romanesque dormitorium (the monks' dormitory from the year 1159), as well as the necessarium (the ancient latrine). The oldest preserved cloister in Austria was built in the first third of the 13th century; its architectural highlight is the hexagonal well house and the monastery's art collection houses unique treasures. *Easter–Oct daily 10am–3pm, longer in summer | 9 euros | Stift Zwettl 1 | www.stift-zwettl.at*

ZWETTL BREWERY

One of the few remaining private breweries (since 1708). Visitors are initiated into the secrets of lager, pilsner and dark beers on 'sundowner' tours *(reservation necessary | 3 hrs). Evening tours every Tue 6.30pm; in summer, also Thu 6.30pm | 14.90 euros | Syrnauer Straße 22–25 | tel. 02822 50 00 | www.zwettler.at*

FOOD & DRINK

WALDVIERTLER STUBEN ☺

High-class village inn with pine-panelled dining room and idyllic guest garden. Most of the food served comes from the region: Waldviertel carp, Waldviertel poppy seed and Waldviertel potatoes (don't forget; they are known as Erdäpfel (earth apples) and not Kartoffeln in the Waldviertel) from the village that are transformed into incredibly fluffy dumplings here. Around 9km (5.5mi) from Zwettl. *43 rooms | Friedersbach 53 | tel. 02822 7 75 11 | www.faulenzerhotel.at | Moderate*

SHOPPING

SONNENTOR ☺

Johannes Gutmann, a child of the Waldviertel, started marketing biologically
produced herbs and spices, some of
which he mixed as teas, around 25 years
ago. He chose the brand name of *Sonnen-
tor (Sun Gate)* and this has now become
well known throughout Austria – today,
he is supplied by around 150 farmers. All
of the products can be bought in his new
shop in Zwettl. *Dreifaltigkeitsplatz 1 | www.
sonnentor.at*

SPORTS & ACTIVITIES

The Waldviertel is perfectly organised for
all kinds of leisure-time sports: mountainbike tours, hiking trails and cycle paths have
been established and signposted. This is
also an ideal region for cross-country skiing

in winter. The topography up here (people
say it is because the Waldviertel is on a high
plateau) is gentle and perfect for those
who are not especially fit. Tour number 55
INSIDER TIP the Hundertwasserweg
(16.5 km/10.2mi | 5.5 hrs), which starts
at the brewery (follow tour 52 for a short
distance) and then continues along the
most wildly romantic section of the Kamp
River until it reaches the old hut that
Hundertwasser used as a refuge for some
time, is actually more of a stroll than a
hike. You will be amazed at the moss-
covered granite boulders in the water
and should keep your eyes open for
mythical figures.

BATHING

On no account, should you miss out on a
visit to one of the nearby Kamp reservoirs
if the weather is sunny enough. If you
stop at the small beach by the Lichtenfels

BOOKS & FILMS

▶ **Desire & Delusion** – Viennese novel-
ist and playwright, Arthur Schnitzler
(1862–1931) is one of Austria's most
respected novelists and playwrights.
Desire and Delusion brings together
three novellas: 'Dying', 'Flight into
Darkness', and 'Fraulein Else'.

▶ **The Piano Teacher** – This novel by
Elfriede Jelinek, who was awarded the
Nobel Prize for Literature in 2004, is a
fine example of Austria's contemporary
classics.

▶ **Sound of Music** – Music and beautiful
mountain scenery set against the ugliness
of the Second World War. Based on the
memoirs of Maria von Trapp and with

lyrics by Oscar Hammerstein, this film
starring Julie Andrew plays on every
Austrian cliché!

▶ **Amadeus** – This period drama play
depicts the life of Amadeus Mozart
from the perspective of his arch rival
Antonio Salieri. Directed by Milos
Forman, the film was awarded
numerous prizes, including eight
Academy Awards.

▶ **Before Sunrise** – A 1995 romance
set in Vienna; Jesse Wallace (Ethan
Hawke), a young American, and Céline
(Julie Delpy), a young French woman,
meet and end up wandering around
Vienna all night talking.

ruins on Lake Ottenstein, you will feel almost like you are in Sweden.

WHERE TO STAY

HOTEL SCHWARZ ALM

This mountain lodge on a romantic clearing in a dense forest once served the brewery horses as a grazing pasture. It has since been converted into an impressive hotel with a fabulous swimming pond. From here, it is only a five-minute walk to the Kamp River where you can wander at leisure for hours in unspoiled nature. Excellent kitchen. *40 rooms | Almweg 1 (5km/3mi from Zwettl) | tel. 02888 5 31 73 | www. schwarzalm.at | Moderate*

INFORMATION

Tourismusmarketing Zwettl: Sparkassenplatz 4 | tel. 02822 50 31 29 | www.zwettl. info; Waldviertel Tourismus: Sparkassenplatz 4 | tel. 02822 5 41 09 | www.waldviertel.at

WHERE TO GO

BLOCKHEIDE GMÜND ●
(134 A2) (*∅ N1*)

The town of Gmünd on the Czech border has a fascinating main square lined with magnificent houses decorated with graffiti. However, Gmund is most famous for its so-called *Blockheide (Block Heath)* where massive granite blocks – with unique, often spherical shapes – are heaped up between the birch groves, red pine and heather. The most spectacular are the *Wackelsteine (wobbling stones)*; forms weighing tons that are delicately balanced on each other and can easily be moved. The most spectacular ones are in the Blockheide *Nature Park*, which is made accessible through a series of hiking trails and where there is also an observation tower. *www.blockheide. at. 26 km (16mi) from Zwettl*

The fortified walls of Rappottenstein Castle

RAPPOTTENSTEIN (134 A3) (*∅ N2*)

The Waldviertel is castle country and the most impressive of all is *Rappottenstein (guided tours daily 11am, noon, 2 and 4pm | 9 euros | www.burg-rappottenstein.at),* which fittingly towers over an almost Medieval landscape. Some of the walls Rapoto von Kuenring had built on the massive granite block are five meters thick. They are arranged in such a way that the inner section of the castle can only be reach by passing five forecourts and eight gates. The keep and pentagonal tower are from the early years of Rappottenstein (12th century); the Renaissance loggia in the innermost courtyard and the sgraffito painting on the windows are particularly impressive. *16km (10mi) from Zwettl*

STYRIA/ CARINTHIA

Austria's south begins at the Semmering Pass and ends at the border to Italy and Slovenia. Styria and Carinthia become more and more pampered by the sun the farther south you proceed.

In southern Styria, that is a great benefit to the wine that grows there and in Carinthia – one of the smaller provinces with an area of 3681mi² and a population of 558,000 – to the lovers of waters sports as the almost 200 lakes reach a temperature of 25°C (77°F) and more. Summer takes place on the lakeside in the southernmost province. Carinthia not only has the warmest lakes but also the highest mountain. That opens up enormous pos-

sibilities and it is easy to combine water and mountain sports in one holiday. On one day, holidaymakers can hike through peaceful valleys into the mountains and swim in the crystal clear water of a lake on the next.

Styria, with a population of 1.2 million and an area of 6309mi², making it the second largest province after Lower Austria, can keep up with its neighbour in the south in terms of contrasts. The northern border is formed by mountains but further south in the Graz Basin it opens up into the hilly landscape of the South and West Styrian wine-growing regions that remind many people of Tuscany. In addition to skiing

Photo: South-Styrian Wine Route showing a klapotetz in the vineyard

Bordering Italy and Slovenia, south-east Austria provides balm for the soul with its rolling green fields and sparkling lakes

areas, spa resorts and the province capital Graz, Styria has many other highlights waiting to be discovered.

BAD AUSSEE

(140 B1) (*∅ L5*) **This spa town (pop. 4900), which was invested with the title of 'Bad' at the end of the 19th century,** **considers itself the capital of the 'inner' Salzkammergut. Here people are proud of their heritage and enjoy wearing their national costume.**

In days gone by, salt – 'white gold' – brought prosperity and high standing to the region, but today the Aussee district lives from its summer flair. The magnificent buildings such as the sgraffito house, the old stone mill, the Meran

The procession of boats decorated with flowers at Altaussee's Narcissus Festival

House and the salt-works hospital whose church is decorated with a Gothic winged altarpiece from 1499, bear witness to the former wealth. The people living here are especially proud of the fact that the town lies in the geographic centre of Austria.

SIGHTSEEING

AUSSEER KAMMERHOFMUSEUM

The 600-year-old so-called Kammerhof where the salt-mine administration was housed in former times is now a local heritage museum with an enormous collection of traditional costumes and a fine speleological section. The Imperial Hall with its Gothic frescoes is also well worth seeing. *June–Sep daily 10am–noon, 3–6pm, May and Oct Tue/Sat 4–6pm, Fri/Sun 10am–noon | entrance fee 4 euros | Chlumeckyplatz 1*

FOOD & DRINK

INSIDER TIP BLAA ALM

Forest inn (5km/3mi). Game and alpine ox specialities. Meals are served on the terrace or in the cosy *Stüberl*. You can try crossbow shooting in the 'Schützenstube'; Tue (from 7pm) folklore evening with music. *Daily | Lichtersberg 73 | Altaussee (towards the Loser Panoramastraße) | tel. 03622 71102 | www.blaa-alm.co.at | Moderate*

KNÖDLALM

Traditional guesthouse, distiller and bio-farm rolled into one. Here, the *knödel* (dumplings) can be savoury or sweet. There are also daily specials such as *Ofenrohrbradl* (roast pork) or roast lamb. This is all accompanied by home-made juice and *schnapps*. *Mon–Wed closed, Thu from 8pm folk music | Knoppen 3 | Pichl-Kainisch (9km/5½mi) | tel. 03624 21132 | www.urig.at | Budget*

WHERE TO STAY

APPARTMENT OASE ☺

This was originally the first handicapped-accessible permaculture complex in Europe to be operated completely organically. The modern wooden cubes of the panorama apartments that followed later fit perfectly into the complex. *12 units | Sigmund Freud Straße 222 | tel. 03622 5 42 45 | www.oase-berta.at | Budget*

ERZHERZOG JOHANN

Comfortably decorated and furnished rooms with private balcony; each room has an individual flower or herb motto. First-class spa and excellent gourmet restaurant. *62 rooms | Kurhausplatz 62 | tel. 03622 52 50 70 | www.erzherzogjohann.at | Expensive*

SHOPPING

● Traditional clothing and old handicrafts can be seen in every second shop window in the charming centre of town; many articles are made in the ☺ immediate vicinity, some of them using methods that have been handed down from generation to generation such as Sepp Wach's hand-printed silk goods *(Bahnhofstr. 108)*.

INFORMATION

TOURISMUSVERBAND AUSSEERLAND-SALZKAMMERGUT
Bahnhofstr. 132 | tel. 03622 54 04 00 | www.ausseerland.at

WHERE TO GO

ALTAUSSEE (140 B1) (*ঞ K5*)

The lake at the foot of the Sandling, the most productive salt mine in Austria, is crystal clear and very refreshing. It can be fun to go rowing on, or hiking around, the lake even if the weather is less than perfect. There is now a model mine *(www.salzwelten.at)* where salt has been extracted since the 8th century. Sturdy shoes and warm clothing are necessary for the two-hour tour through the galleries, over slides and past the Barbara Chapel. *4.5 km (3mi) from Bad Aussee*

DACHSTEIN ★ (140 A2) (*ঞ K5*)

With its 2995m (9826ft), the Hohe Dachstein is the highest peak in the massif of the same name. The ascent with the ☈ glacier railway past the almost perpendicular south wall is an unforgettable experience in itself. The ☈ *Sky Walk* with its glass floor that juts out over the edge of the 250m (820ft)-steep cliff at the mountain station is spectacular. You can

---

★ **Dachstein**
Sensational panorama, glacier railway and Sky Walk – also accessible for tourists in sandals
→ p. 89

★ **Admont Monastery**
Benedictine abbey from the 11th century with a fascinating library, monastery experiential world and modern art → p. 90

★ **South-Styrian Wine Route**
The wine-growing area on the Slovenian border makes visitors almost feel like they are in Tuscany → p. 96

★ **Hochosterwitz**
The picturesque fifteenth-century castle on a 175m (574ft)-high dolomite cliff near Klagenfurt served as a model for Disney films → p. 99

MARCO POLO HIGHLIGHTS

walk a short distance through the glacier in the *Dachstein Eispalast* but it is also possible to make a regular glacier hike along a prepared path that leads to the Dachsteinwarte in around one hour. *www.derdachstein.at | valley station in Ramsau. 75km (47mi) from Bad Aussee*

GRUNDLSEE (140 B1) *(㎿ L5)*
The largest lake in Styria in front of the impressive setting of the Dachstein is very popular with anglers, yachtsmen, surfers and divers. A short path from Gößl on the east shore leads to the *Toplitzsee*. It has a fairy-tale setting and has become legendary because it is believed that the Nazis sunk treasures in it during the Third Reich – so far, nothing has been found. The *Fischerhütte* prepares delicious char from the lake *(Wed closed | Moderate). 5km (3mi) from Bad Aussee*

OEDENSEE 😊 (140 B1) *(㎿ L5)*
The Oedensee (with a lovely hiking trail) in the district of Pichl-Kainisch is a very lovely stretch of countryside. On a guided tour, you can learn all about the flora and fauna of the region and then take a break at the *Kohlröserlhütte (daily | Kainisch 144 | tel. 03624 2 13 | Budget)*. The staff in the kitchen of this forest-and-fish restaurant really knows how to prepare Styrian specialities and fish from the local lakes and rivers. *8 km (5mi) from Bad Aussee*

ADMONT MONASTERY ⭐
(141 D1) *(㎿ M5)*
It is something of a miracle that the library of this Benedictine monastery from 1074 remained preserved after a fire. It is the largest monastery library in the world. The fresco on the ceiling was created by Bartolomeo Altomonte. Today, the monastery is famous for its collection of contemporary – mostly Austrian – art and its modern monastery experiential world that gives multimedial impressions of cloistered life *(mid-March–Nov daily 10am–5pm | entrance fee 9.50 euros | www.stiftadmont.at)*. Admont is at the entrance to the Gesäuse National Park. This is where the River Enns cut a valley through the alpine world leaving steep rock faces of up to 1800m (5905ft) in height in its wake – it goes without saying that this is an excellent area for hiking and climbing *(www.nationalpark.co.at). 63km (39mi) from Bad Aussee*

GRAZ

(142 B4) *(㎿ O6–7)* The second largest city in Austria (pop. 297,000) has experienced a boom in modernisation in recent years that reached its peak in 2003 when Graz was European Capital of Culture.
The island in the Mur River and the Kunsthaus are architectural witnesses to these developments. The special flair of Graz is mainly a result of its southern location, mild climate, magnificent Renaissance palaces and, not least, the many students in the city. The old city was named a Unesco World Heritage Site in 1999 on account of it being the 'largest medieval town centre in the German-speaking world'. The two central green areas on the Schlossberg and in the Stadtpark (City Park) make a great contribution to the

> **CITY WHERE TO START?**
> There is a good view from the **Schlossberg** (Castle Mountain). After you have oriented yourself, take a relaxed stroll down to the city and start your tour of its sights. Tramlines 4 and 5, which travel through Graz from north to south, take you straight to the Schlossberg.

The futuristic island in the River Mur, the Kunsthaus and inner city of Graz

quality of life in Graz. On your stroll through the Styrian capital, you should take a look at one or more of the many inner courtyards. There, time seems to have come to a standstill and you will really enjoy breathing in the relaxed, southern atmosphere that can be felt in them.

SIGHTSEEING

CATHEDRAL

The church, which was first mentioned in 1174 and rebuilt in the 15th century, was formerly connected to the court and only named a bishop's church in 1786. The 'Landplagenbild' (Plague Picture) by Thomas von Villach (1485) on the outside is especially noteworthy. *Bürgergasse*

ISLAND IN THE MUR RIVER

The American Vito Acconici placed a multifunctional construction of interlinked mussel-formed components made of steel, chrome and glass in the River Mur that open up new vistas of the city and river. The island is accessible. *Franz-Josefs-Kai/Lendkai*

JOANNEUM

The Joanneum Museum is one of the oldest public institutions of its kind in Austria; it developed out of the extensive scientific collection of Archduke Johann and has glowed in modern splendour since his 200th birthday (2011). The core is formed by the Museum of Natural History – 400 million years of the history of the (Styrian) earth on two levels *(Tue–Sun 10am–5pm | Joanneumsviertel | 8 euros | www.museumjoanneum.at)*. Schloss Eggenberg, whose astronomical originality makes it another part of Graz's Unesco World Heritage, is also administered by the Joanneum *(daily | Eggenberger Allee (with tramline number 1) | 8 euros, combi-ticket with the Joanneum 11 euros)*.

The magnificent arcaded courtyard of the Landhaus in Graz

KUNSTHAUS

The Kunsthaus on the banks of the Mur was opened in 2003 and soon developed into a contemporary symbol of the city. The two London architects Peter Cook and Colin Fournier created a fascinating artistic space with their very innovative language of forms. *Tue–Sun 10am–5pm | entrance fee 8 euros, combi-ticket with the Joanneum 11 euros| Lendkai 1 | www.kunsthausgraz.at*

LANDHAUS (PROVINCE PARLIAMENT)

The Renaissance building with its cool arcades and three-storey courtyard, where the Styrian Parliament meets, was created in the middle of the 16th century by Domenico d'Allio and is the city's greatest architectural gem. Concerts are frequently held in the courtyard in the evening. The round-arch portal at the entrance on Schmiedgasse dates back to 1494.

MAUSOLEUM OF FERDINAND II

The striking tomb with its three domes was created by Pietro de Pomis between 1614 and 1638. After the death of the em-peror, the interior was decorated following plans drawn up by Bernhard Fischer von Erlach; it is easy to recognise the transition from the Renaissance to Baroque periods. *Bürgergasse near the Cathedral*

SCHLOSSBERG

The 473m (1552ft)-high Schlossberg, or castle hill, is dominated by the clock tower. The symbol of Graz from the year 1561 is also the best-preserved section of what was the city fortress. You should definitely make sure that you have enough time for a stroll on the Schlossberg – start at Karmeliterplatz; it is quicker with the funicular railway *(bottom station Kaiser-Franz-Josef-Kai)*, and even quicker if you take the lift from Schlossbergplatz.

FOOD & DRINK

DER STEIRER

Classical restaurant, dead-smart wine bar and modern sales counter rolled into one. Down-to-earth cooking that leaves INSIDER TIP plenty of room for surprises – the menu lists Graz capon – a rooster rubbed with anchovies and stuffed with a filling of bread rolls and liver – alongside the traditional deep-fried chicken. *Daily | Belgiergasse 1 | tel. 0316 70 36 54 | www.der-steirer.at | Moderate*

MOHRENWIRT

Traditional inn with simple food focusing on meat. It is just as simply decorated; nothing has changed for a good forty years. But, there is nowhere where you can eat more authentically – Graz hospitality since 1586! *Thu/Fri closed | Mariahilferstr. 16 | tel. 0316 71 20 08 | Budget*

STAINZERBAUER

Creative, refined Styrian cuisine is served in one of the oldest restaurants in Graz, and the wine list is among the best in town! Charming guest garden in the Renaissance inner courtyard. *Daily | Bürgergasse 4 | tel. 0316 82 11 06 | Moderate*

SHOPPING

Fresh products from the surrounding district are sold every day at the *Kaiser-Josef Market* behind the Opera and *Farmers' Market on Lendplatz*; Styrian pumpkin seeds and the dark-green oil made from them are two of the top products. If you don't have time to travel along the South-Styrian Wine Route, you can taste and stock up on wine and other specialities at the *Vinofaktur (daily 10am–10pm, Sun from 11am | Belgiergasse 1).*

ENTERTAINMENT

Graz's nightlife is colourful and extremely varied. The fashionable places are concentrated in the area of the inner city between the four squares Haupt-, Mehl-, Glockenspiel- and Freiheitsplatz. It is easy to find exactly what you are looking for in the vaults of the Cuban *Café Bar Continuum (Sporgasse 29)*, in the INSIDERTIP lovely inner courtyard of *Las Tapas (Sporgasse 11)* or over a glass of prosecco in the *Aiola City (Mehlplatz 1)*. Those who are more romantic can ride or walk up the Schlossberg where the observation terrace of the *Aiola Upstairs* will invite them to gaze at the stars. After a visit to the opera or theatre, many Grazers traditionally go to the *Theatercafé (Mandellstr. 11)*; it is famous for its different varieties of scrambled eggs *(Eierspeis)*. Excellent cabaret performances are given on the café's own stage from September to May.

WHERE TO STAY

DAS WEITZER

The top dog among the hotels in Graz is the time-honoured Weitzer on Grieskai – and there is no alternative for those looking for a laid-back, cool, trendy hotel at

LOW BUDGET

▶ You can live extremely well at extremely affordable prices in the holiday homes operated by *Landlust* – the rural houses are at least 100 years old and have been stylishly renovated. A holiday dwelling for two can be had for as little as 40 euros a day. *www.landlust.at*

▶ Camping is an obvious choice for holidaymakers staying by the Carinthian lakes. There are countless camping grounds at beautiful locations with direct access to the water. An estimated 50 of them also offer bungalows and mobile homes for around 40 euros a night for two persons.

a reasonable price. *202 rooms | Grieskai 12–16 | tel. 0316 70 30 | www.weitzer.com | Moderate*

INSIDER TIP ▶ HOTEL DANIEL

This is where the new 'Budget & Design' concept was realised: functional, attractive, chic, relaxed and affordable. *107 rooms | Europaplatz 1 | tel. 0316 7110 80 | www.hoteldaniel.at | Budget–Moderate*

PALAIS-HOTEL ERZHERZOG JOHANN

This opulent city palace in a top location was transformed into a hotel back in 1852. Everything here is in the best of taste – antiques, genuine carpets, parquet floors – and underlines the feeling of being in an aristocratic residence. Very pleasant atmosphere, charming attentive service and spacious rooms. *59 rooms | Sackstr. 3–5 | tel. 0316 81 16 16 | www.erzherzog-johann. com | Expensive*

INFORMATION

GRAZ INFORMATION

Herrengasse 16 | 8010 Graz | tel. 0316 8 07 50 | www.graztourismus.at | www. steiermark.com

WHERE TO GO

BAD RADKERSBURG (142 C5) (*ω P7*)

The small town (pop. 1360) lies directly on the Mur River and the border to Slovenia where the former suburbs spread out. Bad Radkersburg was established in the 13th century as a fortress against the Hungarians. This defensive character becomes particularly obvious when you approach the *city wall* from the spa centre and it looms up in front of you. It has been almost completely preserved and protects a gem of historical architectural art. The second major attraction of Bad Radkersburg is the *spa*. This is the place to enjoy a warm bath and the water is particularly beneficial for people suffering from problems with their musculoskeletal system. *www.badradkersburg.at | 80km (50mi) from Graz*

HARTBERG (142 C3) (*ω P6*)

People have been living in the region around the 'East Styrian metropolis' for a good 3000 years. Historical sights waiting to be discovered in the idyllic inner city include sections of the impressive city wall, such as the impressive *Reckturm* in the castle park and the *Schölbingerturm* by the town pond, the *castle* of the later lords of the castle at the upper end of the park, the *parish church* that was restyled in the Baroque period with the Hartberg charnel house and its brightly coloured frescoes, as well as the town hall from 1898 on the main square. You will be able to find out more about the history of Hartberg in the *Museum (Wed–Sun 10am–4pm | entrance fee 4 euros | Herrengasse 6).* The *Vinothek Pusswald (Sun/Mon closed. | Grazer Str. 18 | tel. 03332 6 25 84 | www.restaurant-pusswald.at | Moderate–Expensive)* serves fabulous Styrian-Asian-Mediterranean food. *62km (39mi) from Graz*

LIPIZZANERWELT PIBER
(142 A4) (*ω N6*)

The federal stud farm in Piber has been the home of the Lipizzaner horses since 1920. This is where the famous white stallions are bred and trained before they make their way to the Spanish Riding School in Vienna. The horse are brown when they are born and only turn white later – you will be able to see that yourself when you watch the mares and their foals enjoying their carefree summer life on the wide meadows. *Visits to the stud farm April–Oct daily 9.30am–5pm, guided tours on the hour (except at noon), Nov–March tours daily 11am and 2pm | entrance fee 12 euros | www.piber.com. 50km (31mi) from Graz*

The famous Lipizzaner horses enjoy life on the meadows of the stud farm in Piber

RIEGERSBURG (142 C4) (*P7*)

The 850-year-old fortress and symbol of East Styria can be seen from afar on top of a 482m (1581ft)-high volcanic cliff. Its history is closely associated with the persecution and condemnation of 'witches' (*Hexenmuseum/Witch Museum*). The Knights' Hall with its beautiful woodwork is especially worth seeing (*May–Sep daily 9am–5pm, April/Oct from 10am / entrance fee 10 euros / www.veste-riegersburg.at*). The 🕐 INSIDER TIP *Schokoladenmanufaktur Josef Zotter* at the foot of the castle hill is famous both for its hand-made chocolate dreams that are produced entirely using Fairtrade ingredients and for all of the entertainment that accompanies their manufacture. In addition, it has created valuable workplaces in a region with a weak infrastructure (*Schokotheater Sun closed / www.zotter.at*). 63km (39mi) from Graz

SCHLOSS HERBERSTEIN
(142 C3) (*P6*)

From a distance, impressive Schloss Herberstein looks more like a citadel that has been forced into the narrow Feistritz Ravine close to the popular Stubenbergsee than the garden castle it is today. Although it is privately owned, it can be visited. Wander through the beautiful garden, the Gironcoli Museum with works by the modern artist Bruno Gironcoli and the *Zoo* with 130 animal species from all over the world. *Castle: Oct–April at least on weekends 10am–4pm; in summer daily / 14.50 euros / www.herberstein.co.at. 33 km (21mi) from Graz*

STAINZ (142 A5) (*O7*)

West-Styrian Schilcherland, named after the wine produced from the Blaue Wildbachrebe grape that is only grown here, spreads out between Stainz and the fortress city of Deutschlandsberg. The acidy, rosé coloured Schilcher is very fashionable at the moment. You can eat well at the 🕐 *Rauch-Hof (Mon/Tue closed / Wald 21 / tel. 03463 28 82 / www.rauch-hof.at / Moderate)* where most of the ingredients come from local producers. The best way to explore Schilcherland is to drive from Stainz to *Rassach* 5km (3mi) away and then on to the *Reinischkogel (www.schilcher land.com)*. 33km (21mi) from Graz

SOUTH STYRIAN WINE ROUTE ⭐
(142 B5–6) (⌀ O6–7)

This route is located deep in the south of Styria on the border to Slovenia and is made up of a network of roads, paths and tiny trails that leaves plenty of room for visitors to make their own discoveries – wine taverns and hikes through the vineyards, wine directly from the grower, hotels run by winegrowers, restaurants. You will come across all of these if you start out in Gamlitz (wine-growing museum in the castle, *www.melcher.at*) and travel on to *Leutschach*. On your way back, make a detour to Langegg where you will be amazed at the sensational architecture of the wine cellars of top winegrower *Sabathi (Pössnitz 48 | www.sabathi.com)* and then, only a few kilometres further on, be rewarded with a wonderful panoramic view of the gently rolling hills that reminds many people of Tuscany from ⋇ *Pössnitzberg*. Finally, a tip for a snack (strudel!): INSIDER TIP ⮞ Buschenschank *Germuth (Thu–Sun from 2pm | Glanzer Kellerstr. 34).* You can get maps from all of the local information offices or, in advance, from *Steiermark Tourismus (tel. 0316 4 00 30 | www.steiermark.com). 55 km (34mi) from Graz*

KLAGENFURT

(140 C5) (⌀ M8) The spacious Neue Platz (New Square) with its commanding patrician houses and the Lindwurm Fountain in the middle is the heart of the Carinthian capital city (pop. 94,300).
The Alte Platz (Old Square) is lined with impressive Baroque buildings and the old town hall and there are many houses from the latter part of the 19th century and Jugendstil period on Kramergasse. You should allow yourself plenty of time for a stroll through the city because the his-torical passages and picturesque inner courtyards will make you want to stop and take a closer look at them. In summer, much of the activity moves to nearby Lake Wörth (Wörthersee).

SIGHTSEEING

CATHEDRAL CHURCH
The earliest pilaster church in Austria was built by protestant groups at the end of the 16th century. It was handed over to the Jesuits in 1604 and then served the Bishops of Gurk as their cathedral church starting in 1787. Visitors' attention is mainly drawn to the surrounding galleries and the majestic high altar with a painting by Daniel Gran (1752) and a picture of Christ by Paul Troger. *Domplatz*

LANDESMUSEUM RUDOLFINUM
The neo-Renaissance building houses a collection of exhibitions concentrating on the region with prehistoric finds, minerals and many exhibits dealing with the history of the city. The Großglockner has been newly staged as a multimedia experiential world. *Tue–Fri 10am–6pm, Thu 10am–8pm, Sat/Sun 10am–5pm | entrance fee 7 euros | Museumgasse 2*

LANDHAUS
(LOCAL PARLIAMENT)
The main attraction of this secular building with two stair turrets and an arcaded courtyard that was constructed in the 16th century is the famous Hall of Arms with a ceiling painting by Joseph Fromiller and the 650 coats of arms of the former territorial estates. *April–Oct Mon–Sat 9am–5pm | entrance fee 3 euros | Landhausplatz*

LINDWURM MONUMENT
The symbol of the city on the Neue Platz in Klagenfurt was created in the year 1590. The lindworm was modelled on the skull

It spurts water, not fire; the Lindwurm on Neuer Platz in Klagenfurt

of a woolly rhinoceros that was found nearby and thought to be the head of a dragon. The figure of Hercules and the iron fence were added in the 17th century.

ROBERT·MUSIL·LITERATUR-MUSEUM ●

The museum in the house where this major figure in world literature and modernist writing was born is devoted to his work, as well as that of two other prominent Carinthian authors, Christine Lavant and Ingeborg Bachmann. *Mon–Fri 10am–5pm | free admission | Bahnhofstr. 50 | www.musilmuseum.at*

FOOD & DRINK

BIERHAUS ZUM AUGUSTIN

Two bars in the long vaulted rooms, beer that really goes down well and down-to-earth, inexpensive food – it comes as no surprise that the *Augustin* has become a popular meeting place. *Mon–Sat from 11am | Pfarrhofgasse 2 | tel. 0463 51 39 92 | Budget*

INSIDER TIP DER HÖHENWIRT 🙂 ☀

The view from the Pyramidenkogel across Wörther See is breathtaking. Take the time to travel the 13km (8mi) to Keutschach to enjoy the fresh cooking with local products in the restaurant that has been decorated with so much care. In addition, there are freshly caught fish and also beautiful rooms for an overnight stay. *(Moderate). Easter–Oct daily, telephone at other times | Pyramidenkogel 4 | Keutschach am See | tel. 04273 23 28 | Moderate*

DOLCE VITA

This elegant Italian restaurant is the best in Klagenfurt. The menu lists fresh fish and seafood (caught and not farmed!). *Mon–Fri 11.30am–3pm and 6pm–midnight | Heuplatz 2 | tel. 0463 5 54 99 | www.dolce-vita.at | Expensive*

SHOPPING

Most of the boutiques can be found near the Alter Platz and also in the passages and inner courtyards. 🙂 Klagenfurt's

Hochosterwitz Castle dominates the landscape near St Veit from a limestone cliff

farmers' market in the centre of town on *Benediktinerplatz (Thu, Sat)* offers a colourful supply of fresh, regional products.

SPORTS & ACTIVITIES

There is hardly any kind of sport that cannot be carried out in the area around the leisure-time paradise of Wörthersee. The most popular are swimming, sailing, surfing and hang-gliding but there are also four golf courses *(www.woerthersee.com)*.

ENTERTAINMENT

The main hots pots for nightlife are on the shores of Wörthersee where the *Casino Velden* is the centre of interest for socialites. The more romantic get together to chill out in the INSIDER TIP *Lido Lounge (Friedelstrand 1)* right on the waterfront. The *Discoclub Custo* at Herrengasse 12 *(Fr/Sa)* has become a meeting place for the beautiful people of the city within a short time. The *Pub Einstein (Paracelsusgasse 14)* is the place to go if you are looking for something a little more peaceful.

WHERE TO STAY

DER SANDWIRTH

A private hotel in the upper 4-star category in the centre of Klagenfurt with very personal service. *100 rooms | Pernhartgasse 9 | tel. 0463 5 62 09 | www.sandwirth.at |* *Moderate*

INFORMATION

KLAGENFURT TOURISMUS
Neuer Platz 1 | 9010 Klagenfurt | tel. 0463 5 37 22 23 | www.klagenfurt-tourismus.at

WHERE TO GO

FRIESACH (140 C4) *(ᗯ M7)*
The oldest town in Carinthia (first mentioned around 860) was once under the jurisdiction of the prince-archbishops of Salzburg and was a very prosperous trading centre in the Middle Ages. The Bartholomäuskirche (St Bartholomew Church), the St.-Josefs-Kloster (St Joseph's Monastery), die Deutschordenskirche (Church of the Teutonic Order) and the

Lavant Castle ruins are proud witnesses to Friesach's heyday. There are spectacular views of the city and into the wide Metnitz Valley from the ☌ *Petersberg* and *Virgilienberg*. A festival is held in the castle every year. *43km (27mi) from Klagenfurt*

GURK (140 C4) (*ω M7*)

The Romanesque basilica from the 12th century is one of the most magnificent churches in the entire province. The highlights include the Romanesque crypt with 100 columns, the Gothic and Renaissance frescos as well as Raphael Donner's Baroque main altar. *38km (24mi) from Klagenfurt*

HOCHOSTERWITZ ★ ☌ (141 D5) (*ω M7*)

Walt Disney was so impressed by this fortress that he used it as a model for his fairy-tale comics. Walk up past the 14 gates and you will be rewarded with a magnificent view over the countryside and be able to visit the impressive armoury. The small town of St Veit an der Glan not far away attracts many visitors with its 200m-long and 30m-wide main square with some of the most beautiful Medieval buildings imaginable. *April–Oct from 9am| 13.50 euros with lift | www.burghochosterwitz.at. 20km (12mi) from Klagenfurt*

ST PAUL (141 E5) (*ω N8*)

Although the Benedictine monastery of St Paul im Lavanttal, which was founded in 1091, does not appear very interesting from the outside, its INSIDER TIP curiosity cabinets and picture gallery house many artistically and historically priceless treasures including works by Rubens, Dürer, Holbein and Kremser Schmidt. The Romanesque pilaster basilica, with the Gothic vaults that were added after a fire in 1367, is especially impressive. Rooms can be rented in the monastery *(Monastery Museum | May–Oct Tue–Sun 9am–5pm). Entrance fee 10.50 euros | www.stift-stpaul. at. 55km (34mi) from Klagenfurt*

WÖRTHERSEE (LAKE WÖRTH) (140 C5) (*ω L8*)

Wörthersee, which is connected to Klagenfurt by the Lendkanal, has few cold water mountain inflows so that the water can reach a temperature of up to 28°C (82°F) in summer. Where Gustav Mahler once found inspiration for his compositions and where films were made and schmaltzy songs written, the beach-volleyball crowd now display their six-packs and the Wörthersee Festival focuses on dance and musicals. Woods reach all the way down to the water on the south side. The Baroque church on the picturesque promontory of Maria Wörth is a popular place for weddings. Those who want to avoid the hustle and bustle in Krumpendorf, Velden and Pörtschach can cycle around the lake; they will need around four hours for the barely 40km (25mi) long trip. *www. woerthersee.com | Velden is 22km (14mi) from Klagenfurt*

VILLACH

(140 B5) (*ω L8*) **Carinthia's second largest town (pop. 64,700), a major transport junction, was heavily bombed during the Second World War.**

Therefore, with the exception of a few town houses on the main square, very little of the old city has been preserved. This is more than made up for by the many lakes – Faaker, Ossiacher and Millstätter Lakes – in the surroundings. The Romans settled where the Gail flows into the Drau River, built bridges and recognised the quality of the thermal springs in Warmbad Villach.

SIGHTSEEING

ST JAKOB'S PARISH CHURCH
The basilica, with its three naves and elaborate net vaulting, the stone pulpit from the year 1555, a Gothic baptismal font and the St Christopher fresco attributed to Thomas von Villach, is definitely worth a visit. *Kirchplatz 8*

FOOD & DRINK

KAUFMANN & KAUFMANN ☺
The ambience is sophisticated, the excellent cuisine inspired by the Mediterranean (with products from the region), and the green inner courtyard just right for romantics. *Sun/Mon closed | Dietrichstein-gasse 5 | tel. 04242 2 58 71 | Moderate*

SPORTS & ACTIVITIES

Spa, sport or would you rather just splash about in the water? The *Kärntentherme*, which was newly opened in 2012, presents itself as a world of fascinating experiences *(www.kaerntentherme.at)*. Of course, most people prefer the nearby lakes *Faaker See* and *Ossiacher See* in summer. The Nock Mountains around Bad Kleinkirchheim and the Nassfeld around Pressegger See, which is a superb skiing area in winter, attract many hikers and mountain bikers *(www.nassfeld.at)*. If you feel your German is good enough, a visit to the comedy performances in the atmospherically illuminated Renaissance *Porcia Castle (www.komoedienspiele-porcia.at)* is a pleasant way to spend an evening in July or August.

WHERE TO STAY

KRAMER
'Der Kramer', as the hotel is called in Villach, is a traditional hotel in the town centre yet still in a green environment. Delightful terrace and small spa. *40 rooms | Italiener Str. 14 | tel. 04242 2 49 53 | www.hotelgasthofkramer.at | Moderate*

INFORMATION

VILLACH-TOURISMUS
Bahnhofstr. 3 | 9500 Villach | tel. 04242 2 05 29 00 | www.villach.at

WHERE TO GO

GROSSGLOCKNER HOCHALPENSTRASSE (139 E4) *(∭ J7)*
Heiligenblut is one of Austria's most photographed villages: the popular motif shows a slender church tower in front of the snow-covered mountain. At 3798m (12,461ft), the Großglockner is the highest mountain in the country, and the Alpine road, which leads to the foot of the mountain's continuously melting and shrinking Pasterze Glacier was considered one of the technical miracles of the age when it was opened to traffic in 1935. The total length of the pass road to the Pinzgau in Salzburg is 48km (30mi); it has 36 bends, reaches an altitude of 2504m (8215ft) and opens up a view of sixty (!) 3000-metre peaks. En route, you pass through the unique mountain world of the *Hohe Tauern National Park* – a breathtaking picture of flowering alpine meadows, mighty rock faces, permanent ice, marmots and ibexes – until you reach the ● observation platform at the Kaiser-Franz-Josefs-Höhe. *Closed in winter from around Oct.–May | 32 euros per car | www.grossglockner.at. 130km (81mi) from Villach*

MILLSTÄTTER SEE (140 A4–5) *(∭ K7)*
The second-largest lake in Carinthia is 12km (7.5mi) long and lies embedded between mountains and hills, which the

Memories of Venice: landing stages on Millstätter See

locals refer to as 'Nocken'. Hiking and swimming are the stars on the programme in this region. At your feet when you INSIDER TIP walk along the Höhenweg, you will see a fairy-tale, densely wooded landscape with the dark water of the lake glittering in between. This is a fine place to go hiking or mountain biking and, of course, for all kinds of water sports – swimming, rowing, surfing, water skiing... Accommodation tip: ☺ Biobauernhof Burgstaller high up in the mountains in an absolutely peaceful location with a view of the lake (Laubendorf 1 | Millstatt | tel. 0699 10 19 83 80 | www.urlaubambauern hof.at/burgstaller | Budget). www.mill stättersee.com. 42km (26mi) from Villach

INSIDER TIP NATURARENA
WEISSENSEE ☺ (139 F5) (*Ø K8*)
At an altitude of 930m (3051ft) above sea level, this lake has the cleanest water in the Alps; it is turquoise blue and reaches a temperature of up to 24°C (75°F) making it ideal for swimming. Two thirds of the shore are not built up at all. Here, you can choose between hiking, running, Nordic walking, mountain biking, swimming, surfing, diving and canoeing. The region has won an EU award for tourism and the environment. Each accommodation provider on Weissensee has his own bathing beach and this is also an ideal place for ice skating in winter. The ☺ Biohotel Gralhof (16 rooms | Neusach 7 | tel. 04713 22 13 | www.gralhof.at | Expensive), an age-old family property that has been turned into a dreamy ecological hotel, can be fully recommended for those who want to spend some time here. 70km (43mi) from Villach

OSSIACHER SEE (140 B5) (*Ø L8*)
In contrast to Wörthersee, Ossiacher See is more suitable for a holiday with the family. Many of the Carinthian Summer Festival concerts are held in the Baroque monastery church in Ossiach. If you take the panoramic railway up to the 🌿 view-point on the Gerlitzen, you will see Carinthia spread out below you. 14km (9mi) from Villach

TRIPS & TOURS

The tours are marked in green in the road atlas, the pull-out map and on the back cover

1

CYCLE TOUR ALONG THE BORDER

Lower Austria's tranquil north with its gentle topography is an ideal place for long cycle tours. The recommended route along the River Thaya covers 66km (41mi) and can be taken at a leisurely pace; it will lead you from the mystical landscape of the Waldviertel (wood quarter) along the Czech border to the gently rolling hills of the Weinviertel (wine quarter). It offers the greatest variety away from the beaten tourist paths for those with only a limited amount of time at their disposal.

The starting point is in **Raabs an der Thaya** that you can reach by taking the post bus from Horn (*www.postbus.at*). Located in a shallow valley at the confluence of the German and Moravian Thaya Rivers, Raabs was founded where old trading routes crossed as a bulwark against the north; the massive castle that dominates the small town is an impressive reminder of those days. You reach **Drosendorf**, today's destination, after a short 12.5km (8mi) ride. The town in rich in history; completely surrounded by a town wall, it can only be entered through the city gate – this is something lovers of old, intact city centres will delight in.

Photo: Flowery meadow in Hinterbichl in the Virgen Valley, Tyrol

A difficult choice: cycling in the east, hiking in the Hohe Tauern Mountains or driving through the Bregenz Forest

Do a INSIDERTIP canoe tour on the Thaya to experience the river you will be following for the next days from a completely different perspective *(canoes can be hired from the Reiterhof Thayatal, Ernst Resl | tel. 0664 2 40 62 49 | 18 euros per day | www.reiterhof-thayatal.at)*. You can eat and sleep well in the *Gasthof Hammerschmiede (15 rooms | www.hotel-hammer schmiede.at | Budget)*.

On the following day, there are 24.5km (15mi) on the programme, most of them along quiet side roads and country lanes. Forests and meadows, ponds and villages will accompany you on your journey and it is well worth making a stop to visit the **Baroque Riegersburg Castle** → p. 94 *(daily 9am–5pm | entrance fee 10 euros | www.riegersburg-hardegg.com)* as well as INSIDERTIP Austria's only *mother-of-pearl* *turnery* in **Felling** *(Mon–Thu 9am–noon and 1–4pm, Fri 9am–noon, April–Oct also Sat 9am–noon | entrance fee 2.50 euros | www.perlmutt.at)* along the way.

Just before you reach **Hardegg**, you come to the dense forest of the trans-border **Thayatal National Park** whose landscape is shaped to a large degree by the meanders of the River Thaya. We would recommend that you do without your bicycle for the next couple of hours: after you reach the bridge in Hardegg, follow the Thayatalweg number 1 path and walk to **INSIDER TIP** Umlaufberg, from where you have the most beautiful view over the idyllic river valley *(3 hours)*. On your return, stop for a visit at the *Maximilian von Mexiko Museum (daily 9am–5pm | entrance fee 8.80 euros)*. A pleasant place to spend the night at the foot of Hardegg Castle is *Gasthof Hammerschmiede* where you can also eat very well *(5 rooms | tel. 02949 82 63 | www.gasthof-hammerschmiede. com | Budget)*.

On the last day of this tour, you bid farewell to the Waldviertel and roll down into the vineyards of the Weinviertel. After pedalling for 15.5km (9.5mi) you arrive in **Retz**, one of the loveliest towns in the Weinviertel. The *Marktplatz (Market Square)*, with the *Stadtturm (City Tower)* with the Renaissance helmet dominating it, is quite magnificent. This is also the entrance to the **Retzer Erlebniskeller** (Retz Experiential Cellar), a 20km (12.5mi)-long subterranean labyrinth built into the soft sand *(Guided tours daily 2pm, May–Sep also 10.30 and 4pm | entrance fee including wine tasting 9.50 euros | entrance: Hauptplatz 30)*.

You can take the bus from Retz back to Horn or add a few kilometres to those you have already covered in order to be able to experience some more of the undulating Weinviertel: from here, the scenery changes in a flash – vineyards take the place of forests and the villages have the typical cellar lanes. With a little bit of luck,

The area above the Umbal Falls in the Virgen Valley is perfect for hiking

the *heuriger* in the *Jetzelsdorf Cellar Lane* in **Haugsdorf** will be open *(www.toiflwein. at)* to make a perfect finish to the tour. Bus connection back to Horn.

The route follows the **Kamp-Thaya-March Cycle Path** that runs for 420km (260mi) through north-eastern Lower Austria near the three rivers that have given it its name. If you want, you can extend the tour in both directions. The *bikeline cycle tour guide 'Kamp-Thaya-March-Radweg'*, which can be ordered from *Weinviertel Tourismus (10.90 euros plus postage | tel. 02552 35 15 | www.ktm-radweg.at,)* is a valuable companion on this trip. You can get more detailed information on the region from: *Tourismusverband Thayatal (tel. 02846 3 65 20 | www.thayatal.com)*.

2   TREKKING FROM HUT TO HUT IN THE NATIONAL PARK

You can find lonely alpine landscapes that have almost been untouched by man not far from cable-car mountain stations. To experience this, sling your rucksack over your shoulder and head off on a trekking tour and spend the nights in mountain huts. The tour we suggest here can only be made between mid-June and September and will take you to the high alpine regions of the Hohe Tauern National Park where you will have three days of unforgettable impressions.

The beginning will take the most out of you; the first thing you have to do is get from the valley to the top and, this time, without a cable car. Take the direct route from **Prägraten** *(1312m/4304ft)* through the romantic *Zopanitzen Valley* to the *Bergerseehütte*, which you should reach after two and a half hours and where you can take accommodation for the night *(2182m/7159ft | tel. 0664 4 33 83 33 | members.aon.at/bergerseehuette)*.

You can spend the rest of the day at the lake – taking a Kneipp cure in the water will bring new life to your weary legs. You might prefer to INSIDER TIP fish for char; the staff in the hut will be delighted to prepare any you catch Or you might decide to spend the afternoon climbing to the peak of the *Bergerkogel (2650m/8694ft)*, from where you will have the entire Virgen Valley spread out at your feet *(ascent 1 hour)*.

If you are a newcomer to hut life, you will be speechless when you wake up the next morning: the first breakfast in the mountains in the glow of the rising sun with nothing but nature around you is an unforgettable experience. But save a few ohs and ahs; you will need them on the next section of this tour that takes you over the spectacular *Muhs Panoramaweg*. Here, you will be overwhelmed by the unique panoramic vista of the entire glacier and mountain world of the Großvenediger, Großglockner and Lasörling group of mountains with background music supplied by the shrill whistling of the marmots and chamois; there is no chance that you won't come across them. Follow the *Micheltalscharte* and *Rote Lenke* and after around five hours you will eventually arrive at the *Neue Reichenberger Hütte*, your destination for today *(2586m/8484ft | tel. 04873 55 80 | www.neue-reichenberger huette.at)*.

You can choose between taking it easy or setting off to conquer another peak in the afternoon; the people who run the hut will be pleased to give you tips. The next day begins with another mind-blowing alpine breakfast followed by the most beautiful stretch of the entire tour: INSIDER TIP the route around the *Rosen- spitze* to the *Clarahütte (2038m/6686ft | 3.5 hours)*. In some sections it is so quiet that you really can hear the silence. Metre-thick fields of snow glitter as white patches in deep rifts. Here, the mountain takes on the gentle shapes of a high plateau; sheep graze in slightly swampy grasslands kept moist by countless rivulets, while the chamois show what they think of gravity as they clamber around the almost perpendicular rock faces.

After some refreshments in the *Clarahütte* – you might be lucky enough to see some ibexes; there is a large colony of them here – the trail widens to become a well-trodden gravel path along the river that makes its way down to the valley over the mighty steps known as the *Umbal Waterfalls* as far as **Ströden**. In the meantime, you have left the solitude of the mountains behind you – the *Wasserschaupfad* is a popular excursion destination. It is only twenty minutes from the end of the Schaupfad to the post bus stop to Ströden from where you can catch the bus back to Prägraten.

Make sure you take along enough sun and rain protection, a (full) water bottle, walking sticks, good maps, a sleeping bag and possibly ear plugs for the nights spent in a dormitory, but still try to keep your backpack as light as possible. An excellent overview of the region with good descriptions of the huts can be found at *www.virgentaler-huetten.at* under *Lasörlingweg*; the *Virgentaler Hüttenbuch* pamphlet can be ordered from the 'hut telephone': *04877 5100*. And please, only set off to do this tour if the weather is fine!

3 · A PLEASURE TRIP IN THE BREGENZ FOREST

The Bregenz Forest displays gentle contours when compared with the rugged high alpine regions of Vorarlberg, and it is only the mountains in the last part of the tour that reach an altitude of over 2000m (6562ft). This leisurely two-and-a-half day car journey from village to village will introduce you to the many age-old traditions and fascinating modern architecture that go hand in hand in this region. It is only 40km (25mi) from Reifensberg, where this tour begins, to the final destination of Schoppernau so you will have ample time to look, be astounded, enjoy and plenty of opportunities to stretch your legs.

The traditional Bregenz Forest costume is known as a *Juppe*; it is made of linen and a special technique is used to make it shine while keeping it stiff but elastic – you can have a demonstration of this in the INSIDER TIP *Juppenwerkstatt* in **Riefensberg** *(May–Oct Tue, Fri 10am–noon, June–Oct also Fri 2–4pm | entrance fee 3 euros| www.juppenwerkstatt.at)*. The house in which the workshop is located was once a barn and is also well worth seeing; it will give you a foretaste of the modern wooden architecture of the Bregenz Forest, something the area is just as famous for as it is for its cheese. The second station in **Lingenau** *(10 km/6mi)* is devoted to the dairy product: the ● *Käsekeller (Mon–Fri 10am–6pm, Sat 9am–5pm | www.kaesekeller.at)* is housed in a monolithic construction of exposed concrete. This is where you will be able to watch a robot taking care of the cheese and buy fine mountain cheese that, here in the Bregenz Forest, is made from milk from cows that get non-silage food – so-called *Heumilch* (hay milk) – which explains its wonderful aroma.

Just 3km (2mi) farther on you reach **Egg**, where Ingo Metzler makes fabulous cosmetics from goat-milk whey and has set up a barn that can be visited as well as a *Sennereischule (Dairy School) (tel. 05512 30 44 | www.molkeprodukte.com)*. There is a wide choice of visits that must be booked in advance. After that, you will have time to have a hearty lunch in the

INSIDER TIP *Gasthof Tonele*, which is famous in Vorarlberg for its delicious *Käsespätzle (reservations recommended, tel. 05512 23 27)*. Pleasantly satisfied, you head to **Andelsbuch** *(3 km/2mi)*, where there is a presentation of all of Vorarlberg's traditional handicrafts in the brand-new and very striking *Werkraum Haus (Sun closed | www.werkraum.at)*. The day comes to an end in **Schwarzenberg → p. 36**, one of the most beautiful of all the villages with wooden architecture; you can spend the night in authentic style in the *Gasthof Hirschen (33 rooms | tel. 05512 29 44 | www. hirschenschwarzenberg.at | Moderate– Expensive)*, which has already notched up 250 years and where you will be able to have an exceptionally fine meal.

The distances to be covered on the next day are even shorter; you reach **Bezau** after a mere 7km (4.5mi) where we recommend that you stay in the *Hotel Post (58 rooms | tel. 05514 2 20 70 | www.hotel postbezau.com | Expensive)*; its interior design is the result of regional craftsmanship. The spa cosmetics are totally natural products from the village of Egg and the entire building is a wonderful example of wooden architecture. As soon as you have checked in, drive to the *Schönenbach car park* and lace up your hiking boots. People only live in **Schönenbach** from June to September and it is considered one of the **INSIDER TIP** *loveliest Vorsäß settlements*. A *Vorsäß* is a meadow half way up the mountain – three-stage agriculture is carried out in the Bregenz Forest; the farmers move their animals up the mountain as the year progresses and this led to its inclusion in Unesco's immaterial world heritage list in 2011. The signposted hike takes around three-and-a-half hours and you will discover magnificently located high-alpine meadows where you will more than likely be offered some cheese. If you are still hungry after this

This is where it matures: cheese from the Bregenz Forest

hike, the *Gasthof Egender* in Schönenbach is a good place to have a bite to eat.

The last day spent in the Bregenz Forest takes you to **Schoppernau** *(17km/10.5mi)*. Here, you can visit the *Franz Michael Felder Museum (Mon 4–6pm, Thu 9–11am, Fri 5–7pm, Sun 9.30–11.30 am)*; Felder was a local nineteenth-century writer, educator and social reformer. The last stop on your trip to all the pleasures of the Bregenz Forest is the *Gasthof Gämsle (Mon closed | www.gaemsle.at | Moderate)*, where you will also find excellent accommodation if you decide to stay longer.

You can find more cheese makers, more modern architecture and more hikes on the Internet under *www.bregenzerwald.at*.

SPORTS & ACTIVITIES

No matter whether you prefer skiing in Ischgl or kite surfing on Lake Neusiedl, golfing in the Lafnitz Valley or hiking from hut to hut in the Hohe Tauern Mountains, Austria offers sports and activities galore! The infrastructure is perfect too because the Austrians also like to use their natural surroundings to get out and about. However, beware! What the locals consider a stroll can turn out to be a strenuous tour for tourists. The following sites give information on the range of sporting options available in Austria: *www.bergfex.at*, as well as *www.alpintouren.com*, where there is a high-quality collection of private tour reports (climbing, hiking, biking, ski tours).

CYCLING

The paths along the Rivers Danube, Inn, Mur, Enns, Drau and Traisen, as well as around Lake Neusiedl, promise cycling pleasure without demanding too much muscle power *(www.radtouren.at)*. The alpine regions on the other hand are an El Dorado for mountain bikers; challenging and well signposted and documented. The top regions in Austria are Leogang/Pinzgau (Salzburg, *www.bike-pinzgau.at*), the Salzkammergut (Upper Austria, *www.biken.at*), the Montafon (Vorarlberg, *www.montafon.com*), the Zugspitzarena (Tyrol, *www.zugspitzarena.com*), the Naturarena

---

Photo: White-water rafting

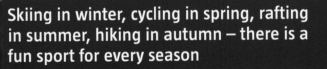

Skiing in winter, cycling in spring, rafting in summer, hiking in autumn – there is a fun sport for every season

(Carinthia, *www.naturarena.com*) as well as the Schladming-Dachstein region (Styria, *www.schladming-dachstein.at*).

GOLF

Almost all of the more than 100 golf clubs have been established in enchanting surroundings; more than a quarter of them are on the plains of Lower Austria, includ-

ing the *GC Schloss Schönborn (tel. 02267 28 79 | www.gcschoenborn.com)*, 45km (28mi) northwest of Vienna that has its clubhouse in a Baroque castle. The three-thousand metre peaks of the Hohe Tauern provide a spectacular backdrop for the golf courses in the Zell am See-Kaprun region *(tel. 06542 56 16 10 | www.golf-zellamsee. at)*. The *Golfschaukel Lafnitztal*, which has more than 50 holes embedded into natu-

Death-defying jumps are an accepted part of extreme skiing

ral surroundings, is more protected from the elements, and it is possible to play there until the middle of November *(www.golf schaukel.at)*. There is an excellent overview of golf in Austria at: *www.golf.at*.

HIKING

In Austria, the chances are good that as soon as you step outside you will find yourself on a hiking trail – and there are always plenty of places where you can stop for a break. Some regions have established groups of 'hiking villages' *(www.wandern-in-oesterreich.at)*. Those interested in cultural history should consider hiking along the Semmering Railway from Lower Austria to Styria. Part of the Way of St James (Camino de Santiago), which has now become popular again, passes through

Austria and covers some of the same route as the Tyrolean *Adlerweg (www.adlerweg. com)*. Other good destinations for treks lasting several days are the Schladminger Tauern Mountains with the *Höhenweg (Peak Path)* and the Dachstein with the eight-day *Dachsteinrunde (www.dachstein rundwanderweg.at)*, which will definitely make you 'glow', the *Almenwanderweg (Alpine Meadow Trail)* in Salzburg *(www. salzburger-almenweg.at)*. Hiking from hut to hut in the Hohe Tauern National Park is a real treat *(see Trips & Tours, p. 105)*.

MOUNTAINEERING & CLIMBING

Expert climbers will find what they are looking for on the Dachstein, in the Gesäuse and on the Wilder Kaiser in Tyrol.

There are literally thousands of routes for all levels of proficiency in western Austria (www.climbers-paradise.com). In addition, there are numerous climbing gardens such as the one on the Kanzianiberg in Carinthia. This is also where the *Outdoorpark Oberdrautal*, which is ideal for newcomers to the sport, is located. The portal for climbers and mountaineers *www.bergsteigen.at* provides an overview and information on routes down to the tiniest detail.

OUTDOOR ACTION

Wildalpen is the place for those proficient at kayaking and canoeing. They can enjoy the challenge of hurling themselves into the white water – the INSIDER TIP Styrian Salza is the longest unspoilt river in Central Europe and can be used all year round (www.wildalpen.at). *Abentau* in the Lammer Valley in Salzburg is the starting point for rafting, canyoning and hydrospeed tours and the mountains in the vicinity offer also excellent conditions for paragliding (www.lammertal.info). The Ötz Valley (www.oetztal.com) and East Tyrol (www.osttirol.com) offer similar action-packed programmes. Classic water sports – windsurfing, kiting, sailing – are just as popular on the lakes in the Salzkammergut as they are on Neusiedler See (www.salzkammergut.at / www.neusiedler see.com). The following websites give full information on the countless outdoor sports possibilities in Vorarlberg and Carinthia: *www.outdoor-vorarlberg.at / www.outdoor.kaernten.at.*

RIDING

Equestrian fans will find perfect conditions for their sport in the Austrian forests and the foothills of the Alps. General information on the various stables is available at:*www.reitarena.com.* Some regions cater especially to horse lovers and have developed networks of riding paths over their hills, meadows and fields; these include the Mühlviertler Alm (www.pferdereich.at), Neusiedler See (www.burgenland.info) and Carinthia, the equestrian's El Dorado (www.reit-eldorado.at).

WINTER SPORT

With the exception of Vienna and the Burgenland, Austria's provinces offer ski resorts with courses for all levels of proficiency. The Montafon and Arlberg in Vorarlberg, Tyrol's Ischgl, Hochgurgl, Hintertux and Kitzbühel, Zell am See-Kaprun, Saalbach-Hinterglemm and die Sportwelt Amadé in the province of Salzburg, the Nassfeld in Carinthia and Schladming in Styria provide skiing circuits with all the bells and whistles. Families often find these mega skiing regions a bit overwhelming; especially when the slopes are full in the high season it can be difficult to keep your eye on everyone. Those who are not sure of themselves on skis or want to ski with their children will probably feel more at home in the smaller regions such as Wildschönau (Tyrol), Weißsee (Salzburg province), Semmering (Lower Austria, Styria) or Hochficht (Bohemian Forest/ Upper Austria). Ischgl and Serfaus in Tyrol, as well as Kleinarl and Piesendorf in the Salzburg mountains are hot spots for fun and games on the slopes. The INSIDER TIP Kreischberg (Murau in Styria) is an insider's tip among snowboarders. In winter, alpine Austria is covered with well-prepared cross-country trails. The centre for skaters, classical cross-country skiers and Nordic ski sport fans in general is in the Ramsau (Styria, www.ramsau.com) and the Bohemian Forest (Upper Austria, www.boehmerwald.at), where a great deal has been invested in a new Nordic Centre in recent years.

TRAVEL WITH KIDS

Clamber up rockfaces, splash around in the lakes, feed the animals on a farm, romp around in the hay and help at harvest time – a holiday in the countryside has many surprises in store every day, especially for children.

As a rule, children will rarely be bored in Austria. There is always a lake nearby for them to go swimming, a farmhouse to spend the night in or a meadow to run about and play. Hikes take them over alpine meadows where dairymen look after their herds and the kids can hear the cows' bells tingling from far away, pony farms that make the youngsters' dream of having a horse of their own come true – at least for a short time. There are lists of hotels that cater especially to children and families under *www.familyaustria.at, www.kinder hotels.com* and *www.familyselect.cc*.

BURGENLAND/VIENNA/ LOWER AUSTRIA

INSIDER TIP **GEOCACHING**

It is possible to undertake an exciting family puzzle-rally with a GPS treasure map, either as a hike or cycle tour, at twenty different points in Lower Austria. The time needed to hike until the treasure is found is 1–6 hours. *Tel. 01 5 36 10 | geocaching. niederoesterreich.at*

Photo: Holidays on a farm in the Mostviertel

Holidays on a farm, summer toboggan runs and adventure parks: children are made to feel welcome everywhere in Austria

FAMILYPARK NEUSIEDLER SEE
(135 E6) *(ØØ Q4)*

If you visit Austria's largest amusement park, the little ones will be absolutely delighted with the fairy-tale forest and the farm with the petting zoo. The more daring will take a ride on the family roller coaster the *Götterblitz (Lightning of the Gods)*, will be whisked up into the air in the Dragon of the Lake, take the apple-tree merry-go-round or throw themselves into the fun in the water with the flying fish. *March–Sep daily 9am–6pm, Oct 10am–5pm | entrance fee 18 euros, children under the age of 3 free | Märchenparkweg 1 | St Margarethen im Bgld. | www.familypark.at*

SONNENTHERME (140 C3) *(ØØ L6)*

The thermal baths in Lutzmannsburg in the Burgenland pay special attention to families with children. In contrast to most other wellness facilities, children are not regarded as a disturbance here – all ages, from babies on, are welcome. The offers are suitably adapted to please the little ones. *Daily 9am–9pm, Fri/Sat to 10pm | day ticket adults 20.40, children 5.70– 12.50 euros (depending on age) | Lutz- mannsburg | www.sonnentherme.at*

ZOOM KINDERMUSEUM
(U B5) (*ⓜ b5*)

This museum just for children in the mu- seum district in Vienna stresses creativity and playful learning. Many different ex- hibitions and ateliers; be sure to book your visit in advance! *Entrance fee be- tween 0 and 6 euros depending on the stations visited | Museumsplatz 1 | www. kindermuseum.at*

STYRIA/CARINTHIA

1. KÄRNTNER ERLEBNISPARK
(1ST CARINTHIAN ADVENTURE PARK)
(139 F6) (*ⓜ K8*)

The park in Hermagor on Pressegger See offers technical attractions such as the jump with the *Nautic Jet*, taming the *Butterfly*, the ride on the *Comet*, hovering with the *Sky Dive* or the excavator simula- tor – and there is a large bathing area on the lakeside. *May–Sep daily 9am–6pm | children from 4 years of age 19, adults from 60, 10 euros | www.erlebnispark.cc*

MINIMUNDUS KLAGENFURT
(140 C5) (*ⓜ M8*)

Show the kids a miniature version of the big wide world; the Minimundus has a display of 150 models of the most beauti- ful buildings from five continents. *April/ Oct daily 9am–6pm, May, June/Sep 9am– 7pm, July/Aug 9am–8pm, Wed to 11pm | entrance fee 13, children (6–15) 8 euros | Villacher Str. 241 | www.minimundus.at*

SUMMER TOBOGGAN RUN
GREBENZEN (140 C3) (*ⓜ M6*)

The 1720m (564ft) make this the longest summer toboggan run in Styria. There are many curves on the way downhill. Comfort- able ride to the top on a four-seat chairlift. *June–Sep daily 9am–5pm | run 7.70, chil- dren 5.10 euros | www.grebenzen.at*

STYRASSIC PARK (142 C5) (*ⓜ P7*)

Bad Gleichenberg attracts its young visi- tors with dinos. In addition to an erupting volcano, there are 80 original-size dino- saurs to be marvelled at. *April–Oct daily 9am–5pm | entrance fee 10, children 6 euros | Dinoplatz 1 | www.styrassicpark.at*

UPPER AUSTRIA/SALZBURG

BAUMKRONENWEG (TREETOP
PATH) ☺ (132 C3) (*ⓜ K2*)

A wooden construction more than 1000m in length has been strung between the treetops. The highlights are the 40m (131ft)-high adventure tower and the tree houses where guests can spend the night. Large playground and forest inn. *April–Oct daily 10am–6pm | children 6–15 years of age 5, adults 8.50 euros | Knechtelsdorf/ Kopfing | www.baumkronenweg.at*

DACHSTEIN CAVES (140 B1) (*ⓜ K5*)

The 'Small Adventure Tour' in the Koppen- brüller Cave near Obertraun, allows chil- dren to discover all the winding paths the water has washed out of the mountain over the past thousands of years. *May– Sep daily 9–4pm with advance reserva- tions | Guided tour adults 26, children 20.50 euros | tel. 05 0140 | www.dachstein- salzkammergut.com*

INSIDER TIP▶ PANNING FOR GOLD
(139 E3) (*ⓜ J6*)

Gold mining has a long tradition in the Rauris Valley. Children can try to strike it rich at three gold-panning sites under the expert guidance of Master Theo Huber. *Naturwaschplatz Bodenhaus-Rauris | June–Sep daily 9.30am–5pm | Fee including equipment 5 euros | tel. 06544 70 52 | www.goldsuchen.at*

KINDERWELTMUSEUM (WORLD OF CHILDREN MUSEUM) (132 B5) (*∅ K4*)

The exhibition at Walchen Castle shows children's lives from the Biedermeier time to the present day. Lachkabinett (Crazy Room), maze, pet zoo, herb trail, barrel slides, balancing and bare-foot path. *May–Sep daily 10am–5.30pm | entrance fee 5.50, children 4.50 euros | www.kinderweltmuseum.at*

TYROL/VORARLBERG

GOLM IM MONTAFON (136 B4) (*∅ B6*)

Jet across the Latschau reservoir on the *Flying Fox*, try to keep your balance way up in the air in the Waldseilpark, race down into the valley on the two-seat *Alpine Coaster* sled – the kids' courage really gets put to the test here. *Combi-*ticket incl. uphill trip 31, children 21.30 euros | www.golm.at*

KING-SIZE LUDO (139 E5) (*∅ J7*)

It is bad enough losing if you play on a normal-size board, but the *Spiele- und Buchhotel Tschitscher (Tschitscher's Game and Book Hotel)* in East Tyrol has a giant version of the German variant of ludo. *Nikolsdorf 21 | tel. 04858 82 19 | www.spielehotel.at*

INSIDER TIP ▶ MURMLIWASSER (137 D4) (*∅ D6*)

Make models of castles, roads and landscapes – with a mixture of earth, sand and water. Various playgrounds and adventure areas, such as water wheels and gutters, landslide hills, water steps and a hanging bridge, have been set up around the Lausbach near the Komperdell middle station in Serfaus. There is a large open-air enclosure with marmots right next door. *Komperdellbahn Serfaus | June–Oct daily 8.30am–5pm | free admission, return trip to the middle station adults 11, children to the age of 14 8.90 euros | www.sommererlebniswelt.at*

Children's playground with a wonderful mountain panorama in Leogang

FESTIVALS & EVENTS

1 Jan New Year's Day; **6 Jan** Epiphany; **Easter Monday**; **1 May** Labour Day; **Ascension Day**; **Whit-Monday**; **Corpus Christi**; **15 Aug** Assumption; **26 Oct** National Holiday; **1 Nov** All Saints' Day; **8 Dec** Immaculate Conception; **25/26 Dec** Christmas

FESTIVALS & EVENTS

JANUARY/FEBRUARY

▶ *Running of the Pinggalperchten* in Mayrhofen (Ziller Valley), ▶ *Running of the Schnabelperchten* in Rauris and ▶ *Glöcklerlauf* in Ebensee; *Perchten*, frightening fur-covered creatures drive away evil spirits and the winter; ▶ *Hahnenkamm Race:* The biggest ski festival in Kitzbühel – count the VIPs! *www.hahnen kamm.com*; ▶ *Fasching (Carnival)* in Bad Aussee with glittery costumes; ▶ *Imster Fasnacht (Shrove Tuesday in Imst)* with a *Schemenlauf* (Running of the Spectres) *(not every year, www.fasnacht.at)*; ▶ *Scheller-lauf* in Nassereith with spectacular costumes and masks *(every three years,*

www.fasnacht-nassereith.at); ▶ *Telfser Schleicherlaufen (every 5 years, www. schleicherlaufen.at)*; ▶ *Villacher Fasching (www.villacher-fasching.at)*

MARCH/APRIL

▶ *Salzburg Easter Festival:* Palm Sunday to the Tuesday after Easter. *www.osterfest spiele-salzburg.at*

MAY/JUNE

▶ *Narzissenfest (Narcissus Festival)* in Bad Aussee, *www.narzissenfest.at*; ▶ *See-prozession (Procession on the Lake)* in Hallstatt: Corpus Christi procession; ▶ *Wiener Festwochen (Vienna Festival Weeks)*. *www.festwochen.at*; ▶ *Gauderfest:* Tyrol's largest spring festival is held in Zell am Ziller. *www.gauderfest.at*; ▶ *Sonn-wendfeuer (Midsummer Festival)* e.g. Sacred Heart Festival in Tyrol, Mountain Fire in the Salzkammergut and Danube in Flames in the Wachau; ▶ *Life Ball in Vienna:* way-out Aids charity ball with international stars. *www.lifeball.org*

JUNE/JULY

▶ *Jazzfest Wien*, *www.viennajazz.org*;

Austria finds plenty of traditional, cultural and trendy reasons for festivals and other celebrations throughout the year

▶ *Donauinselfest in Vienna:* Europe's biggest open-air event. *www.donauinselfest. at;* ▶ *Styriarte:* Styrian music festival in Graz highlighting Nikolaus Harnoncourt. *www. styriarte.com;* ▶ *Tanzsommer:* Innsbruck becomes the centre of the world of dance. *www.tanzsommer.at;* ▶ *Seefestspiele Mörbisch:* operettas directly on the lake. *www.seefestspiele-moerbisch.at;* ▶ INSIDER TIP *Wellenklänge:* world music in a spectacular setting on Lunzer See. *www.wellenklaenge.at*

JULY/AUGUST

▶ *Impulstanz:* international dance festival in Vienna. *www.impulstanz.com;* ▶ *Glatt & Verkehrt* in Krems: new interpretations of folk music from around the world. *www. glattundverkehrt.at;* ▶ *Salzburger Festspiele: www. salzburgfestival.at;* ▶ *Bregenzer Festspiele: www. bregenzerfestspiele.com;* ▶ INSIDER TIP *Gamsjagatage (Chamois Hunter Days):* traditional festival in the Salzkammergut. *www.gamsjagatage.at*

SEPTEMBER/OCTOBER

▶ *Ars Electronica:* festival for electronic music in Linz. *www.aec.at;* ▶ *Haydn-Festspiele* in Eisenstadt. *www.haydnfestival.at;* ▶ *Steirischer Herbst (Styrian Autumn):* avant-garde art in Graz. *www.steirischer herbst.at;* ▶ *Bauernherbst (Farmers' Autumn)* in Salzburg province, *www.bauern herbst.at;* ▶ *Weinherbst (Wine Autumn),* *www.weinherbst.at*

NOVEMBER/DECEMBER

▶ *Krampusläufe:* Krampus accompanies St Nicholas and punishes bad children; the events in Bad Goisern and Schladming are particularly spectacular; ▶ *Advent-märkte:* the Advent Markets in front of Schönbrunn Palace, on Wolfgangsee and in Velden have a very special atmosphere.

LINKS, BLOGS, APPS & MORE

LINKS

▶ www.tyrol.com Comprehensive portal for Tyrol, providing detailed information on everything from hiking and mountain biking to culture and spa resorts

▶ www.austriatraveldirect.com/tours.php?D=58 An overview of the key culinary specialities awaiting you in Austria and – because nobody just orders coffee in Austria – a short list of the alternatives available

▶ www.traildino.com All you need to know about your destination at a glance: Interactive maps with planning function, impressions from the community, up-to-date news and offers ...

▶ www.volksmusikland.at This hand-picked selection of traditional songs and dances makes it possible to get an acoustic image of the country. Arranged according to categories with a great deal of background information

BLOGS & FORUMS

▶ http://mwurz1975.wordpress.com Matthias Wurz, who was born in Vienna and studied music in England, offers up-to-date cultural and political insights to the Austrian capital

▶ www.austrianfashion.net Public communications platform for the country's couture world with lively discussions on fashion in Austria, as well as interviews, portraits and naturally information and reports on events

▶ www.justlanded.ch/english/Austria/Forums A fairly active forum intended for the English-speaking community living in Austria

Regardless of whether you are still preparing your trip or already in Austria: these addresses will provide you with more information, videos and networks to make your holiday even more enjoyable

VIDEOS

▶ theyshootmusic.at Indie music – videos made at historical and unusual places in Vienna

▶ short.travel/oes1 The song 'Skifoan' by the Austrian pop singer Wolfgang Ambros is one of the country's unofficial anthems; this live performance is backed with pictures of snow-covered mountains

▶ www.tourvideos.com/Austria-travel-videos.html A series of travel videos about Austria to help facilitate decisions for your programme

APPS

▶ Peakfinder This app tells you the name of the individual peaks you can see as a panorama in front of your eyes. Including map with huts

▶ Steirerguide The free app provided by the Styrian Tourist Board is a virtual travel guide – with 360-degree panoramic views of the destinations introduced (sights, food & drink, accommodation, sport & leisure)

▶ iSki Austria Free apps provide details of where to find the best snow and the most exciting ski resorts

▶ South Tyrol Trekking Guide guides you through South Tyrol's most beautiful hiking and trekking tours with detailed maps

NETWORK

▶ www.facebook.com/tirol The federal province with the most fans and correspondingly the greatest number of pinboard entries

▶ freikarte.at Excellent culture calendar with the possibility to win prizes. As a blog on Facebook and Twitter

▶ de-de.facebook.com/winescene News and events concerning various winegrowers

TRAVEL TIPS

ARRIVAL

✈ There are many daily connections from British airports to Vienna and other destinations in Austria (also budget airlines). Flying time from London to Vienna is around two and an half hours. British Airways offer regular flights from the UK to Austria and you can also fly direct with Austrian Airlines *(www.austrian.com)*. Major carriers in the USA and Canada, e.g. United Airlines Delta Airlines and Air Canada also offer flights.

🚗 From the south of England, the main overland route is from Dover via Calais through Belgium (to avoid the motorway tolls) and straight down towards Munich. The best way to reach Salzburg and Carinthia is by motorway from Munich via Rosenheim to Salzburg (A8) or Kufstein (A93). The route from Ulm via Memmingen (A7) to Lindau (A96) is better if your destination is in Vorarlberg. The main road from Innsbruck to Vienna is via the Inntal- and Westautobahn (A1). The Südautobahn (A2) runs from Vienna via Graz to Klagenfurt and Villach. Villach can also be reached via the Tauernautobahn (A10) from Salzburg. *Autobahns* are subject to toll in Austria. The necessary stickers can be bought at tobacconists, post offices and petrol stations near the border. A (reduced price) sticker is also obligatory for motorbikes. Tolls are also charged on many mountain and panorama roads, as well as some of the important transit routes such as the Brenner Autobahn, Gerlospass- and Felbertauernstraße.

🚆 You can also travel to Austria by train *(www.seat61.com)*. The average travel time from London to Vienna is nine hours.

BUS & RAIL

Using public transport in Austria requires a certain amount of planning: smaller villages are frequently only serviced once or twice a day. For information on the network and timetable of the ÖBB (Austrian Federal Railway) contact *(tel. 05 17 17 | www.oebb.at)* and *(tel. 0810 22 23 33 | www.postbus.at)* for post buses.

CAMPING

Many well-run camping facilities are available throughout Austria. Wild camping is forbidden. It is not possible to drive on many mountain roads with a caravan. Information: *The Camping and Caravanning Club | tel. 0845 601 0905 | www.camping andcaravanningclub.co.uk* or in Austria *Österreichischer Camping-Club (ÖCC) | tel. 01 7 13 6151 | www.campingclub.at*

RESPONSIBLE TRAVEL

It doesn't take a lot to be environmentally friendly whilst travelling. Don't just think about your carbon footprint whilst flying to and from your holiday destination but also about how you can protect nature and culture abroad. As a tourist it is especially important to respect nature, look out for local products, cycle instead of driving, save water and much more. If you would like to find out more about eco-tourism please visit: *www.ecotourism.org*

From arrival to weather

Holiday from start to finish: the most important addresses and information for your trip to Austria

CUSTOMS

The import and export of goods for personal use is tax-free within the EU. For example, 800 cigarettes, 200 cigars, 10L of spirits, 90L of wine or 110L of beer are the guidelines. There are lower limits for travellers from non-EU countries: 200 cigarettes or 50 cigars or 250g of tobacco, 2L of alcoholic beverages (up to 15%). U.S. residents please see *www.cbp.gov*

DISCOUNT CARDS

Card mania has broken out in Austria – an increasing number of regions offer tourist cards that can really ease the strain on your holiday budget. On the one hand, there are city cards (Vienna, Linz, Salzburg, Innsbruck), which are also valid for the public transport network, and province cards (Lower Austria and Carinthia); both of which you have to pay for. And, on the other, the free ● regional cards (e.g. Neusiedler See, Schladming-Dachstein, Steierisches Thermenland (Styrian Spa Country), Mostviertel, Wörther See, Millstätter See, Kaprun, Serfaus-Fiss-Ladis) that you are presented with when you stay in one of the partner enterprises. Irrespective of whether you have to pay or not, as a rule, admission to the most important attractions – and sometimes even cable cars – is free.

DRIVING IN AUSTRIA

There is a speed limit of 130kph on the Autobahn, 100kph on national roads and 50kph in built-up areas; the blood alcohol limit is 0.5. It is obligatory to wear a safety vest as soon as you leave the car on the

BUDGETING

Coffee	from £1.90/$3 *for a melange*
Set meal	from £4.60/$7.30 *at lunchtime*
Entrance fee	from £6.50/$10.50 *for a major attraction*
Train ticket	£25.50/$40.50 *e.g. from Vienna–Linz*
Cable car	from £7.30/$11.70 *for an uphill journey in summer*

motorway or dual carriageway. Snow tyres are compulsory from 1 Nov to 15 April if the weather conditions make it necessary. ÖAMTC breakdown assistance: *tel. 120* ARBÖ breakdown assistance: *tel. 123* In the large cities it is a good idea to leave your car parked at the hotel; parking places are hard to find and expensive. Get information about the parking system in the smaller towns you visit; often, only short-term parking is allowed and there are several different methods (ticket machines, pay & display with tickets purchased from tobacconists, or free with a parking disc).

EMBASSIES & CONSULATES

BRITISH EMBASSY IN VIENNA
Jauresgasse 12 | tel. +43 (1) 716130 | www. gov.uk/government/world/austria

U.S. EMBASSY IN VIENNA
Boltzmanngasse 16 | tel. +43 (1) 313 39-0 | austria.usembassy.gov

CURRENCY CONVERTER

£	€	€	£
1	1.20	1	0.85
3	3.60	3	2.55
5	6	5	4.25
13	15.60	13	11
40	48	40	34
75	90	75	64
120	144	120	100
250	300	250	210
500	600	500	425

$	€	€	$
1	0.75	1	1.30
3	2.30	3	3.90
5	3.80	5	6.50
13	10	13	17
40	30	40	50
75	55	75	97
120	90	120	155
250	185	250	325
500	370	500	650

For current exchange rates see www.xe.com

EMERGENCY SERVICE

Ambulance: *tel. 144*, Police: *tel. 133*, Fire brigade: *tel. 122*, Emergency doctor: *tel. 141*, Alpine emergency number (Mountain Rescue Service): *tel. 140*, in Vorarlberg *tel. 144*, Euro emergency number: *tel. 112* The Euro emergency number is toll-free and functions even without a SIM card in your mobile phone.

HEALTH CARE

European residents should present their European Health Insurance Card EHIC. Additional travel insurance is advisable and, of course, for non-EU residents essential.

Remember to ask for receipts for any treatment so that you can apply for a refund from your own health authority upon your return home. U.S. citizens should check with their medical insurance whether it covers them for treatment abroad.

INFORMATION

ÖSTERREICH WERBUNG

www.austria.info; Tel. 00800 40 02 00 00 In addition, the sites run by the tourist organisations of the individual provinces provide excellent information: *www. burgenland.info, www.niederoesterreich. at, www.wien.info, www.steiermark.com, www.kaernten.at, www.oberoesterreich.at, www.salzburgerland.com, www.salzburg. info, www.tirol.at, www.vorarlberg.travel.*

NEWSPAPERS

The two national high-quality newspapers are 'Die Presse' and 'Der Standard'. The 'Salzburger Nachrichten' and 'Falter', which are indispensible if you visit Vienna, have a similar standard. There are several other papers including the 'Kurier' (East Austria), the 'Kleine Zeitung' (Styria, Carinthia), The 'Krone' and 'Österreich'. International newspapers are available in many larger towns and at train stations, airports, etc.

POST

The postage for a standard letter (to 20 g) to anywhere in the EU is 70 cents, worldwide 1.70 euros.

PHONE & MOBILE PHONE

Country code for Austria: *+43*. When calling from abroad, omit the *0* from the dialling code. The mobile phone network in Austria covers the entire country with the exception of some mountainous regions. If you intend to make local calls within Austria, buy a pre-paid card that can be obtained from all mobile-phone providers.

WHERE TO STAY

A large percentage of the accommodation provided in Austria is in easy-going, often traditional, three and four star hotels and guesthouses that can become really large in some of the most popular holiday regions – this is especially true of Tyrol. An increasing number of very trendy, very 🙂 ecologically conscious – and sometimes very expensive – hotels are opening their doors all over the country. The international chains have hotels in the towns but rarely in the countryside. Health resorts (www.relax-guide.at), as well as luxurious castle hotels (www.schlosshotels.co.at) complete the range at the upper end of the scale. At the lower end of the same scale,

you will find many private rooms and holiday flats; you can find out their addresses from the information services of the individual regions or the booking platform www.tiscover.com and make your reservations there. Holidays on farms (www. urlaubambauernhof.at, also on horse, health, herb and 🙂 bio farms as well as in mountain chalets and on wine-growing estates) are inexpensive and will give you a real feeling for the country. The prices in the youth hostels and family guesthouses (www.jufa.eu) are moderate and the accommodation often superb. See also: www. landlust.at (old country houses in eastern Styria), www.burgenland.info/en (follow the link to 'Pannonian living') or www. niederoesterreich.at. Igloo villages in winter are a recent development (www.schnee dorf.com, www.alpeniglu.com, www.iglu-village.at). It is also a good idea to look around at www.austria.info/at.

WEATHER IN VIENNA

	Jan	Feb	March	April	May	June	July	Aug	Sept	Oct	Nov	Dec
Daytime temperatures in °C/°F												
	1/34	3/37	8/46	14/57	19/66	22/72	25/77	24/75	20/68	14/57	7/45	3/37
Nighttime temperatures in °C/°F												
	−4/25	−2/28	1/34	6/43	10/50	13/55	15/59	15/59	11/52	7/45	3/37	−1/30
Sunshine hours/day												
	2	3	4	6	7	8	8	8	7	5	2	1
Precipitation days/month												
	8	7	8	8	9	9	9	9	7	8	8	8

USEFUL PHRASES GERMAN

PRONUNCIATION

We have provided a simple pronunciation aid for the german words
(see the square brackets). Note the following:

ch   usually like ch in Scottish "loch", shown here as [kh]
g   hard as in "get"
ß   is a double s
ä   like the vowel in "fair" or "bear"
ö   a little like er as in "her"
ü   is spoken as ee with rounded lips, like the French "tu"
ie   is ee as in "fee", but ei is like "height", shown here as [ei]
'   stress on the following syllable

IN BRIEF

Yes/No/Maybe	Ja [yah]/Nein [nein]/Vielleicht [fee'leikht]
Please/Thank you	Bitte ['bi-te]/Danke ['dan-ke]
Sorry	Entschuldige [ent'shul-di-ge]
Excuse me, please	Entschuldigen Sie [ent'shul-di-gen zee]
May I ...?/ Pardon?	Darf ich ...? [darf ikh]/Wie bitte? [vee 'bi-te]
I would like to .../	Ich möchte ... [ikh 'merkh-te]/
have you got ...?	Haben Sie ...? ['hab-en zee]
How much is ...?	Wie viel kostet ...? [vee-feel 'koss-tet]
I (don't) like this	Das gefällt mir/nicht [das ge-'felt meer/nikht]
good/bad	gut/schlecht [goot/shlekht]
broken/doesn't work	kaputt [ka-'put]/funktioniert nicht/
	funk-tsion-'eert nikht]
too much/much/little	(zu) viel/wenig [tsoo feel/'vay-nikh]
Help!/Attention!/ Caution!	Hilfe! ['hil-fe]/Achtung! [akh-'tung]/ Vorsicht! ['for-sikht]
ambulance	Krankenwagen ['kran-ken-vaa-gen]/
	Notarzt ['note-aatst]
police/fire brigade	Polizei [pol-i-'tsei]/Feuerwehr ['foy-er-vayr]
danger/dangerous	Gefahr [ge-'far]/gefährlich [ge-'fair-likh]

GREETINGS, FAREWELL

Good morning!/after-noon!/evening!/night!	Gute(n) Morgen ['goo-ten 'mor-gen]/Tag [taag]/ Abend ['aa-bent]/Nacht [nakht]
Hello!/goodbye!	Hallo ['ha-llo]/Auf Wiedersehen [owf 'vee-der-zayn]

Sprichst du Deutsch?

"Do you speak German?" This guide will help you to say the basic words and phrases in German

See you!	Tschüss [chüss]
My name is ...	Ich heiße ... [ikh 'hei-sse]
What's your name?	Wie heißt Du [vee heist doo]/ heißen Sie? ['heiss-en zee]
I'm from ...	Ich komme aus ... [ikh 'ko-mme ows]

DATE & TIME

Monday/Tuesday	Montag ['moan-tag]/Dienstag ['deens-tag]
Wednesday/Thursday	Mittwoch ['mit-vokh]/Donnerstag ['don-ers-tag]
Friday/Saturday	Freitag ['frei-tag]/Samstag ['zams-tag]
Sunday/holiday	Sonntag ['zon-tag]/Feiertag ['fire-tag]
today/tomorrow/ yesterday	heute ['hoy-te]/morgen ['mor-gen]/ gestern ['gess-tern]
hour/minute	Stunde ['shtun-de]/Minute [min-'oo-te]
day/night/week	Tag [tag]/Nacht [nakht]/Woche ['vo-khe]
What time is it?	Wie viel Uhr ist es? ['vee-feel oor ist es]
It's three o'clock	Es ist drei Uhr [ez ist drei oor]

TRAVEL

open/closed	offen ['off-en]/geschlossen [ge-'shloss-en]
entrance (vehicles)	Zufahrt ['tsoo-faat]
entrance/exit	Eingang ['ein-gang]/Ausgang ['ows-gang]
arrival/departure (flight)	Ankunft ['an-kunft]/Abflug ['ap-floog]
toilets/restrooms / ladies/gentlemen	Toiletten [twa-'let-en]/ Damen ['daa-men]/Herren ['her-en]
(no) drinking water	(kein) Trinkwasser [(kein) 'trink-vass-er]
Where is ...?/Where are ...?	Wo ist ...? [vo ist]/Wo sind ...? [vo zint]
left/right	links [links]/rechts [rekhts]
straight ahead/back	geradeaus [ge-raa-de-'ows]/zurück [tsoo-'rük]
close/far	nah [naa]/weit [veit]
taxi/cab	Taxi ['tak-si]
bus stop/ cab stand	Bushaltestelle [bus-hal-te-'shtell-e]/ Taxistand ['tak-si- shtant]
parking lot/parking garage	Parkplatz ['park-plats]/Parkhaus ['park-hows]
street map/map	Stadtplan ['shtat-plan]/Landkarte ['lant-kaa-te]
airport/train station	Flughafen ['floog-ha-fen]/ Bahnhof ['baan-hoaf]
schedule/ticket	Fahrplan ['faa-plan]/Fahrschein ['faa-shein]
I would like to rent ...	Ich möchte ... mieten [ikh 'mer-khte ... 'mee-ten]
a car/a bicycle	ein Auto [ein 'ow-to]/ein Fahrrad [ein 'faa-raat]
a motorhome/RV	ein Wohnmobil [ein 'vone-mo-beel]
a boat	ein Boot [ein 'boat]

petrol/gas station	Tankstelle ['tank-shtell-e]
petrol/gas / diesel	Benzin [ben-'tseen]/Diesel ['dee-zel]
breakdown/repair shop	Panne ['pan-e]/Werkstatt ['verk-shtat]

FOOD & DRINK

Could you please book a table for tonight for four?	Reservieren Sie uns bitte für heute Abend einen Tisch für vier Personen [rez-er-'vee-ren zee uns 'bi-te für 'hoy-te 'aa-bent 'ein-en tish für feer pair-'zo-nen]
The menu, please	Die Speisekarte, bitte [dee 'shpei-ze-kaa-te 'bi-te]
Could I please have ...?	Könnte ich ... haben? ['kern-te ikh ... 'haa-ben]
with/without ice/ sparkling	mit [mit]/ohne Eis ['oh-ne eis]/ Kohlensäure ['koh-len-zoy-re]
vegetarian/allergy	Vegetarier(in) [veg-e-'taa-ree-er]/Allergie [al-air-'gee]
May I have the bill, please?	Ich möchte zahlen, bitte [ikh 'merkh-te 'tsaa-len 'bi-te]

SHOPPING

Where can I find...?	Wo finde ich ...? [vo 'fin-de ikh]
I'd like .../I'm looking for ...	Ich möchte ... [ikh 'merkh-te]/Ich suche ... [ikh 'zoo-khe]
pharmacy/chemist	Apotheke [a-po-'tay-ke]/Drogerie [dro-ge-'ree]
shopping centre	Einkaufszentrum [ein-kowfs-'tsen-trum]
expensive/cheap/price	teuer ['toy-er]/billig ['bil-ig]/Preis [preis]
more/less	mehr [mayr]/weniger ['vay-ni-ger]
organically grown	aus biologischem Anbau [ows bee-o-'lo-gish-em 'an-bow]

ACCOMMODATION

I have booked a room	Ich habe ein Zimmer reserviert [ikh 'haa-be ein 'tsi-me rez-erv-'eert]
Do you have any ... left?	Haben Sie noch ein ... ['haa-ben zee nokh]
single room	Einzelzimmer ['ein-tsel-tsi-mer]
double room	Doppelzimmer ['dop-el-tsi-mer]
breakfast/half board	Frühstück ['frü-shtük]/Halbpension ['halp-pen-si-ohn]
full board	Vollpension ['foll-pen-si-ohn]
shower/sit-down bath	Dusche ['doo-she]/Bad [baat]
balcony/terrasse	Balkon [bal-'kohn]/Terrasse [te-'rass-e]
key/room card	Schlüssel ['shlü-sel]/Zimmerkarte ['tsi-mer-kaa-te]
luggage/suitcase	Gepäck [ge-'pek]/Koffer ['koff-er]/Tasche ['ta-she]

BANKS, MONEY & CREDIT CARDS

bank/ATM	Bank/Geldautomat [bank/'gelt-ow-to-maat]
pin code	Geheimzahl [ge-'heim-tsaal]
I'd like to change ...	Ich möchte ... wechseln [ikh 'merkh-te ... 'vek-seln]

cash/credit card	bar [bar]/Kreditkarte [kre-'dit-kaa-te]
bill/coin	Banknote ['bank-noh-te]/Münze ['mün-tse]

HEALTH

doctor/dentist/	Arzt [aatst]/Zahnarzt ['tsaan-aatst]/
paediatrician	Kinderarzt ['kin-der-aatst]
hospital/	Krankenhaus ['kran-ken-hows]/
emergency clinic	Notfallpraxis ['note-fal-prak-sis]
fever/pain	Fieber ['fee-ber]/Schmerzen ['shmer-tsen]
diarrhoea/nausea	Durchfall ['doorkh-fal]/Übelkeit ['ü-bel-keit]
inflamed/injured	entzündet [ent-'tsün-det]/verletzt [fer-'letst]
prescription	Rezept [re-'tsept]
pain reliever/tablet	Schmerzmittel ['shmerts-mit-el]/Tablette [ta-'blet-e]

POST, TELECOMMUNICATIONS & MEDIA

stamp/letter	Briefmarke ['brief-maa-ke]/Brief [brief]
postcard	Postkarte ['posst-kaa-te]
I'm looking for a prepaid card for my mobile	Ich suche eine Prepaid-Karte für mein Handy [ikh 'zoo-khe 'ei-ne 'pre-paid-kaa-te für mein 'hen-dee]
Do I need a special area code?	Brauche ich eine spezielle Vorwahl? ['brow-khe ikh 'ei-ne shpets-ee-'ell-e 'fore-vaal]
Where can I find internet access?	Wo finde ich einen Internetzugang? [vo 'fin-de ikh 'ei-nen 'in-ter-net-tsoo-gang]
socket/adapter/	Steckdose ['shtek-doh-ze]/Adapter [a-'dap-te]/
charger/wi-fi	Ladegerät ['laa-de-ge-rayt]/WLAN ['vay-laan]

LEISURE, SPORTS & BEACH

bike/scooter rental	Fahrrad-['faa-raat]/Mofa-Verleih ['mo-fa fer-lei]
rental shop	Vermietladen [fer-'meet-laa-den]
lesson	Übungsstunde ['ü-bungs-shtun-de]

NUMBERS

0 null [null]	10 zehn [tsayn]	20 zwanzig ['tsvantsikh]
1 eins [eins]	11 elf [elf]	50 Fünfzig ['fünf-tsikh]
2 zwei [tsvei]	12 zwölf [tsvölf]	100 (ein) Hundert ['hun-dert]
3 drei [drei]	13 dreizehn [' dreitsayn]	200 Zwei Hundert [tsvei 'hun-dert]
4 vier [feer]	14 vierzehn ['feertsayn]	1000 (ein) Tausend ['tow-zent]
5 fünf [fünf]	15 fünfzehn ['fünftsayn]	2000 Zwei Tausend [tsvei 'tow-zent]
6 sechs [zex]	16 sechzehn ['zekhtsayn]	10 000 Zehn Tausend [tsayn 'tow-zent]
7 sieben ['zeeben]	17 siebzehn ['zeebtsayn]	
8 acht [akht]	18 achtzehn ['akhtsayn]	½ ein halb [ein halp]
9 neun [noyn]	19 neunzehn ['noyntsayn]	¼ ein viertel [ein 'feer-tel]

NOTES

FOR YOUR NEXT HOLIDAY ...

MARCO POLO TRAVEL GUIDES

ALGARVE
AMSTERDAM
ATHENS
AUSTRALIA
AUSTRIA
BANGKOK
BARCELONA
BERLIN
BRAZIL
BRUGES, GHENT &
   ANTWERP
BRUSSELS
BUDAPEST
BULGARIA
CALIFORNIA
CAMBODIA
CANADA EAST
CANADA WEST
   ROCKIES
CAPE TOWN
   WINE LANDS,
   GARDEN ROUTE
CAPE VERDE
CHANNEL ISLANDS
CHICAGO
   & THE LAKES
CHINA
COLOGNE
COPENHAGEN
CORFU
COSTA BLANCA
   VALENCIA
COSTA BRAVA
   BARCELONA
COSTA DEL SOL
   GRANADA
CRETE
CUBA
CYPRUS
   NORTH AND
   SOUTH
DUBAI
DUBLIN
DUBROVNIK &
   DALMATIAN COAST
EDINBURGH

EGYPT
EGYPT'S RED
   SEA RESORTS
FINLAND
FLORENCE
FLORIDA
FRENCH ATLANTIC
   COAST
FRENCH RIVIERA
   NICE, CANNES &
   MONACO
FUERTEVENTURA
GRAN CANARIA
GREECE
HAMBURG
HONG KONG
   MACAU
ICELAND
INDIA
INDIA SOUTH
   GOA & KERALA
IRELAND
ISRAEL
ISTANBUL
ITALY
JORDAN
KOS
KRAKOW
LAKE GARDA

LANZAROTE
LAS VEGAS
LISBON
LONDON
LOS ANGELES
MADEIRA
   PORTO SANTO
MADRID
MALLORCA
MALTA
   GOZO
MAURITIUS
MENORCA
MILAN
MOROCCO
MUNICH
NAPLES &
   THE AMALFI COAST
NEW YORK
NEW ZEALAND
NORWAY
OSLO
PARIS
PHUKET
PORTUGAL
PRAGUE

RHODES
ROME
SAN FRANCISCO
SARDINIA
SCOTLAND
SEYCHELLES
SHANGHAI
SICILY
SINGAPORE
SOUTH AFRICA
STOCKHOLM
SWITZERLAND
TENERIFE
THAILAND
TURKEY
TURKEY
   SOUTH COAST
TUSCANY
UNITED ARAB
   EMIRATES
USA SOUTHWEST
VENICE
VIENNA
VIETNAM

MARCO POLO

ROAD ATLAS & PULL-OUT MAP

KE GARDA

BALDO WITH MOUNTAIN BIKE
to Malcesine takes bikes too
ES" IN SALÒ
re "Bacelo"
Insider
Tips

MARCO POLO

With STREET ATLAS & PULL-OUT MAP

EW YORK

, WILD FLOWERS AND SKYSCRAPERS
the High Line in Chelsea

OW CLOUD NINE
er at 230 Fifth Street
Insider
Tips

MARCO POLO

With ROAD ATLAS & PULL-OUT MAP

FRENCH RIVIERA
NICE, CANNES & MONACO

SPECTACULAR GRAND CANYON DU VERDON
Breath-taking scenery that takes spone healing

SNIFFING THE AIR
The perfume manufacturers of Grasse
Insider
Tips

www.marcopolo.com

MARCO POLO

With ROAD ATLAS & PULL-OUT MAP

ALLORCA

N FLAIR IN THE MEDITERRANEAN
lorca's most beautiful beach

N" CROWD MEET
nde in Ibiza
Insider
Tips

MARCO POLO

With STREET ATLAS & PULL-OUT MAP

BERLIN

A STUNNING ISLAND JUST FOR ART
Showcasing treasures from around the world

Y COOL AT NIGHT
rlin club scene sets the trend
Insider
Tips

- PACKED WITH INSIDER TIPS
- BEST WALKS AND TOURS
- FULL-COLOUR PULL-OUT MAP
  AND STREET ATLAS

ROAD ATLAS

Exploring Austria

The map on the back cover shows how the area has been sub-divided

SchafbergBahn

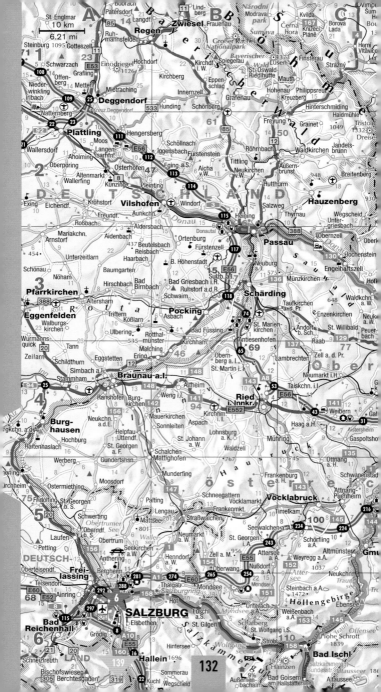

133

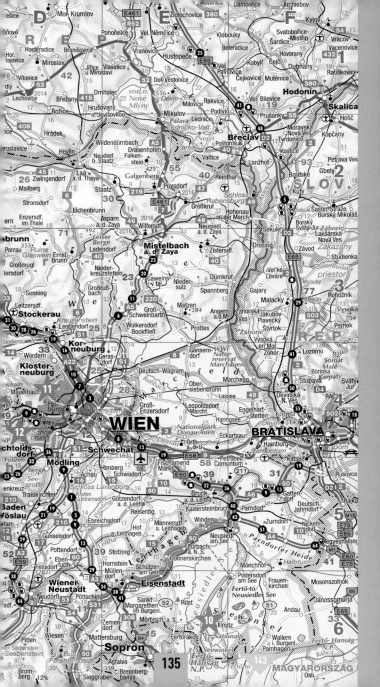

135

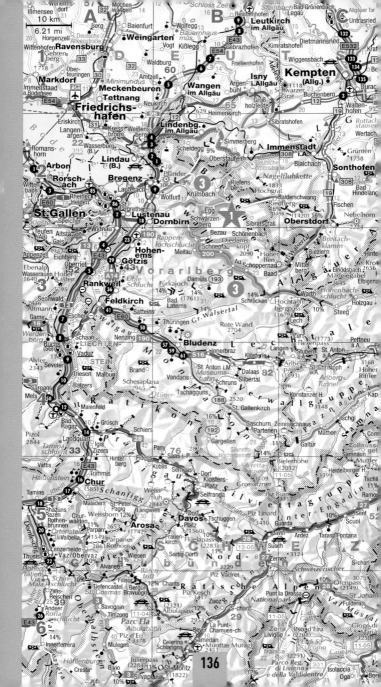

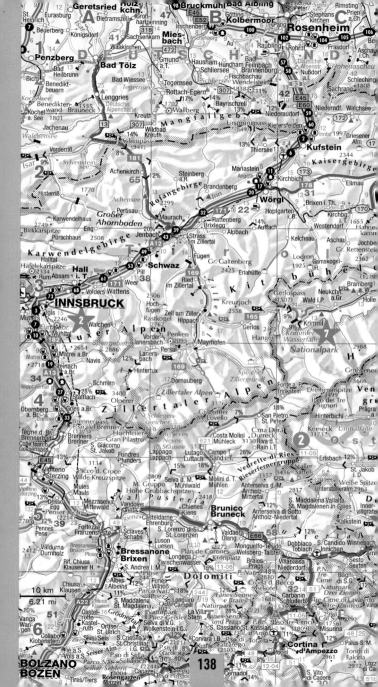

138

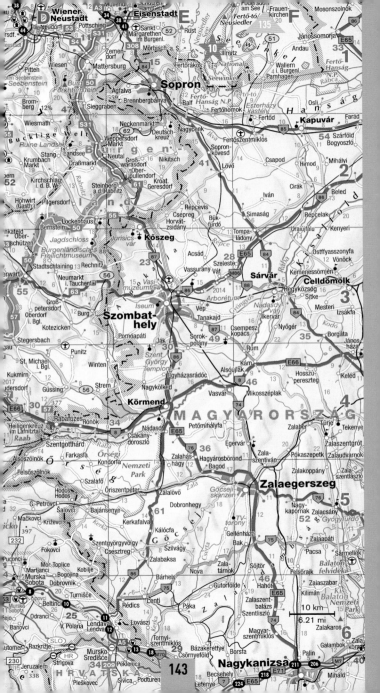

KEY TO ROAD ATLAS

Motorway with junctions
Autobahn mit Anschlussstellen

Motorway under construction
Autobahn in Bau

Toll station
Mautstelle

Roadside restaurant and hotel
Raststätte mit Übernachtung

Roadside restaurant
Raststätte

Filling-station
Tankstelle

Dual carriage-way with
motorway characteristics
with junction
Autobahnähnliche Schnell-
straße mit Anschlussstelle

Trunk road
Fernverkehrsstraße

Thoroughfare
Durchgangsstraße

Important main road
Wichtige Hauptstraße

Main road
Hauptstraße

Secondary road
Nebenstraße

Railway
Eisenbahn

Car-loading terminal
Autozug-Terminal

Mountain railway
Zahnradbahn

Aerial cableway
Kabinenschwebebahn

Railway ferry
Eisenbahnfähre

Car ferry
Autofähre

Shipping route
Schifffahrtslinie

Route with
beautiful scenery
Landschaftlich besonders
schöne Strecke

Alleenstr. Tourist route
Touristenstraße

XI-V Closure in winter
Wintersperre

Road closed to motor traffic
Straße für Kfz gesperrt

8% Important gradients
Bedeutende Steigungen

Not recommended
for caravans
Für Wohnwagen nicht
empfehlenswert

Closed for caravans
Für Wohnwagen gesperrt

Important panoramic view
Besonders schöner Ausblick

* Wartenstein Of interest: culture - nature
* Umbalfälle Sehenswert: Kultur - Natur

Bathing beach
Badestrand

National park, nature park
Nationalpark, Naturpark

Prohibited area
Sperrgebiet

Church
Kirche

Monastery
Kloster

Palace, castle
Schloss, Burg

Mosque
Moschee

Ruins
Ruinen

Lighthouse
Leuchtturm

Tower
Turm

Cave
Höhle

Archaeological excavation
Ausgrabungsstätte

Youth hostel
Jugendherberge

Isolated hotel
Allein stehendes Hotel

Refuge
Berghütte

Camping site
Campingplatz

Airport
Flughafen

Regional airport
Regionalflughafen

Airfield
Flugplatz

National boundary
Staatsgrenze

Administrative boundary
Verwaltungsgrenze

Check-point
Grenzkontrollstelle

Check-point with
restrictions
Grenzkontrollstelle mit
Beschränkung

ROMA Capital
Hauptstadt

VENÉZIA Seat of the administration
Verwaltungssitz

Trips & Tours
Ausflüge & Touren

Perfect route
Perfekte Route

MARCO POLO Highlight
MARCO POLO Highlight

INDEX

This index lists all towns and destinations, plus major lakes and valleys featured in this guide. Numbers in bold indicate a main entry.

WRITE TO US

e-mail: info@marcopologuides.co.uk

Did you have a great holiday?
Is there something on your mind?
Whatever it is, let us know!
Whether you want to praise, alert us
to errors or give us a personal tip –
MARCO POLO would be pleased to
hear from you.
We do everything we can to provide the
very latest information for your trip.

Nevertheless, despite all of our authors'
thorough research, errors can creep in.
MARCO POLO does not accept any
liability for this. Please contact us by
e-mail or post.

MARCO POLO Travel Publishing Ltd
Pinewood, Chineham Business Park
Crockford Lane, Chineham
Basingstoke, Hampshire RG24 8AL
United Kingdom

PICTURE CREDITS
Cover photograph: Lofer, Baroque Maria Kirchental Church, Look/Engel & Gielen
O. Bolch (2 centre bottom, 32/33); Dachstein: Erich Hagspiel (16 bottom, 145); W. Dieterich (28/29); Döllerer
Genusswelten GmbH (17 bottom); DuMont Bildarchiv: (74), Anzenberger-Fink (2 centre top, 6, 26 right, 58, 130/131),
Bernhart (3 bottom, 5, 102/103, 104), Damm (79), Huber (63, 88, 97), Kiedrowski (107), Kreder (9), Mirau (71),
Trummer (2 top, 4, 60), Widmann (53), Wrba (3 top, 12/13, 22/23, 24/25, 64/65, 66, 76, 81, 82); R. Freyer (30
right, 54); R. Hackenberg (3 centre, 21, 29, 69, 86/87, 98, 117, 118 bottom); High end RENT: Susanne Schönherr
(16 top); J. Holz (15, 101); Huber: Dörr (18/19), Gräfenhain (front flap left, 10/11, 41), Mallaun (108/109), Novak
(26 left), Schmid (2 bottom, 28, 45, 48/49), Giovanni Simeone (50, 91); G. Jung (front flap right, 7, 8, 42, 116/117);
Laif: Caputo (116), Huber (112/113), Standl (95); Look: Engel & Gielen (1 top); P. Mathis (34, 36, 110); mauritius
images: ib (Schauhuber) (85), imagebroker.net (38), Mallaun (119); Ploom: Kurt Salhofer (17 top); Schapowalow:
Geiersperger (118 top); T. Stankiewicz (27, 47, 57, 73, 92); W. Storto (115); Darko Todorovic Photography,
Stadtmarketing Bregenz (16 centre)

1st Edition 2014
Worldwide Distribution: Marco Polo Travel Publishing Ltd, Pinewood, Chineham Business Park,
Crockford Lane, Basingstoke, Hampshire RG24 8AL, United Kingdom. E-mail: sales@marcopolouk.com
© MAIRDUMONT GmbH & Co. KG, Ostfildern
Chief editor: Marion Zorn
Author: Siegfried Hetz, co-author: Anita Ericson, editor: Martin Silbermann
Programme supervision: Anita Dahlinger, Ann-Katrin Kutzner, Nikolai Michaelis
Picture editors: Barbara Mehrl, Gabriele Forst
What's hot: wunder media, Munich
Cartography road atlas & pull-out map: © MAIRDUMONT, Ostfildern
Design: milchhof : atelier, Berlin; Front cover, pull-out map cover, page 1: factor product munich
Translated from German by Robert Scott McInnes; editor of the English edition: Sarah Trenker
Prepress: M. Feuerstein, Wigel
Phrase book in cooperation with Ernst Klett Sprachen GmbH, Stuttgart, Editorial by Pons Wörterbücher

DOS & DON'TS

Some tips to avoid unpleasant situations

DON'T ORDER DRINKS THE WRONG WAY

Forget the German you learned at school: In Austria, wine or juice mixed with water is not a *Schorle* but *gespritzt*. *Apfelsaft gespritzt* (half apple juice and half (soda) water) is a refreshing drink in summer; if you just order a *Gespritzen*, you will get a wine-water mixture. This comes in red and white but if you don't specify anything, you will get white! And then there is coffee; there are so many possibilities to get things wrong that you would really need a separate guide book. But don't forget to always stress the second syllable of *Kaffee*.

DON'T DRIVE ON THE AUTO-BAHN WITHOUT A STICKER

A toll must be paid to use the Austrian Autobahns and there can be heavy fines if you are caught without the appropriate sticker. Make sure you buy a sticker – called a *Pickerl* in Austria – that is valid for the whole time you spend in the country *(see p. 120)* because its adherence is rigorously controlled.

DON'T TALK ABOUT FOOTBALL

If you hear the name Cordoba, what do you think about? The city in Spain or maybe the one in Argentina? Austrians, especially male Austrians, think about the 1978 world championship when the national team beat the Germans 3:2 and sent them home. The Austrians did not get any further themselves but they were given a heroes' welcome when they returned to the country. That was probably the last time that Austria was really noticed in international football – today the national team hovers around close to insignificance. But many local fans see things differently and it is probably best to avoid the subject.

DON'T GO INTO THE MOUNTAINS UNPREPARED

If the weather is fine, a hike might seem like a pleasant way to spend the day. But there can be a dramatic change in the weather in the mountains in just a few minutes, and you might find yourself in a dangerous situation if a storm develops or fog falls in. Protection from the rain, warm clothing, a good map and the right shoes are a must if you go hiking, and you should only set out if the weather forecast is favourable – the best idea is to ask the person who runs the mountain hut or a guide. You should also bear in mind that there is often no mobile phone reception in the mountains and you will not be able to send an SOS. And never overestimate your own physical fitness and sure-footedness.

DON'T GET HUNGRY ON SUNDAY

Many inns in rural areas close on Sunday afternoon. As all of the shops are also closed and there are not snack bars everywhere. Often the only option is the expensive shops at a petrol station. Make sure you stock up in advance if you haven't at least booked half board.